Corrective

LIGHTING, POSING & RETOUCHING

FOR DIGITAL PORTRAIT PHOTOGRAPHERS

2nd Ed.

Jeff Smith

AMHERST MEDIA, INC. ■ BUFFALO, NY

Published by:
Amherst Media, Inc.
P.O. Box 586
Buffalo, N.Y. 14226
Fax: 716-874-4508
www.AmherstMedia.com

Publisher: Craig Alesse
Senior Editor/Production Manager: Michelle Perkins
Assistant Editor: Barbara A. Lynch-Johnt

ISBN-13: 978-1-58428-157-3
Library of Congress Control Number: 2004113073

Printed in Korea.
10 9 8 7 6 5 4 3 2 1

Notice of Disclaimer: The information contained in this book is based on the author's experience and opinions. The author and publisher will not be held liable for the use or misuse of the information in this book.

TABLE OF CONTENTS

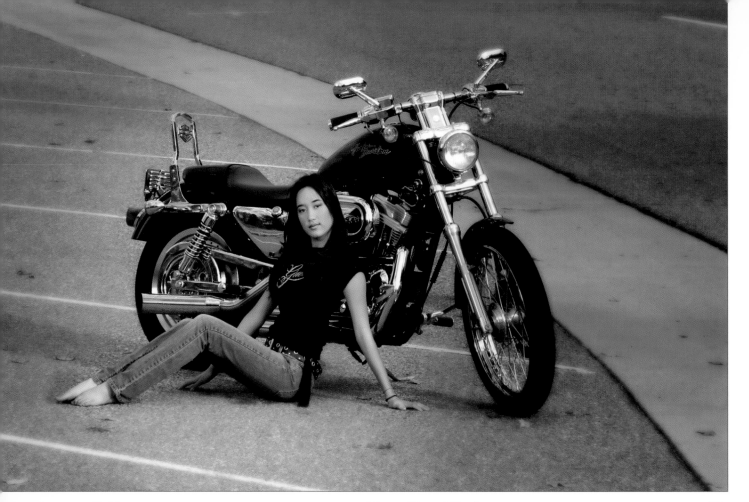

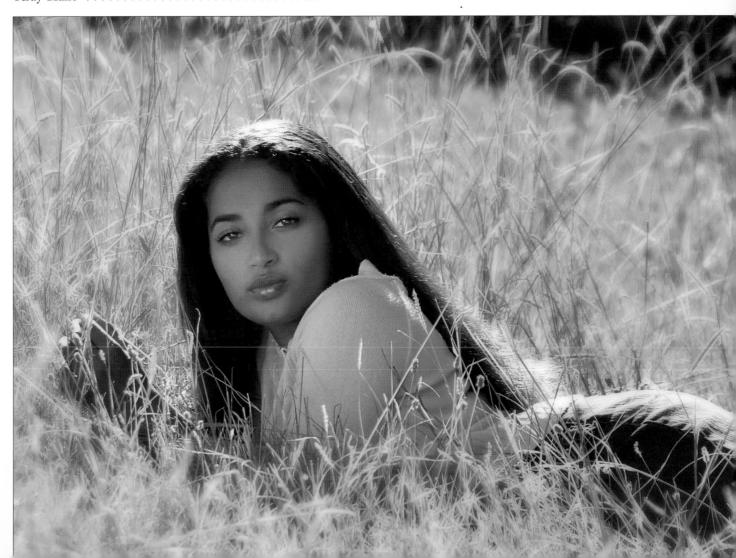

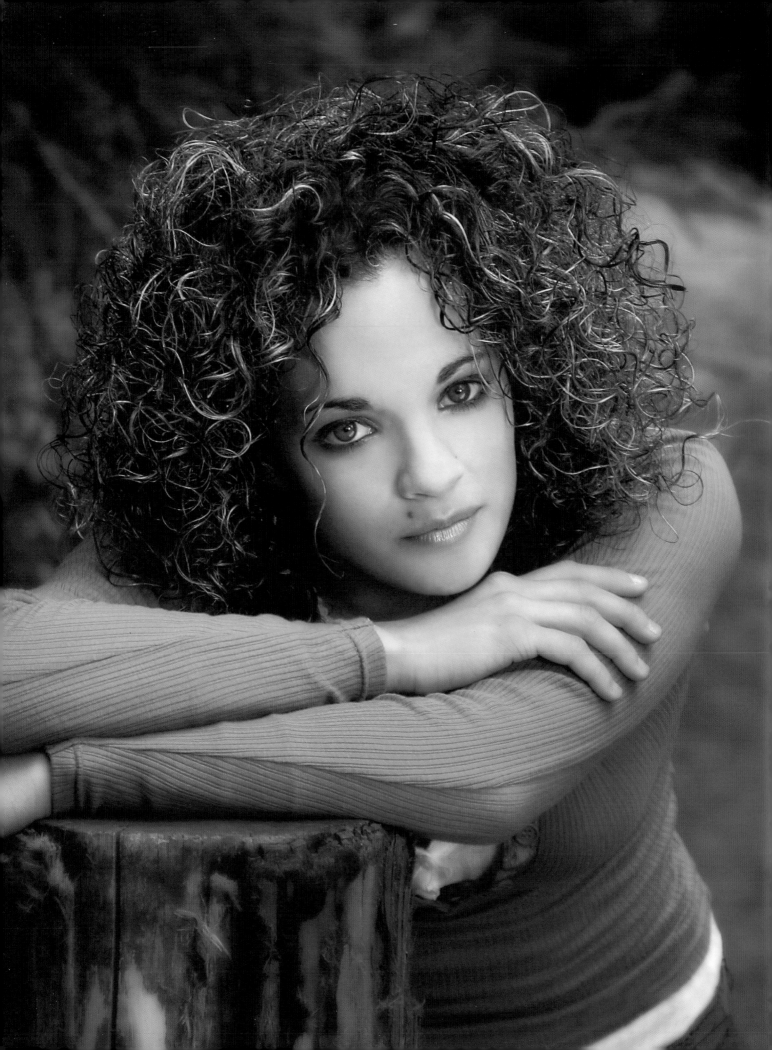

PHOTOGRAPHING REAL PEOPLE

Cameras are designed to record reality—a two-dimensional record of a three-dimensional world. Most photographers start to feel pretty good about themselves when they can, by the proper use of lighting, achieve a portrait that has the appearance of a third dimension. But then what?

Reality, with the appearance of a third dimension, is what the department store and mall photographers give to their clients. They produce images that are a road map of the human face, showing every inch, every

Mall photographers produce images that show every inch, every pore, and every line. Who wants to see all that?

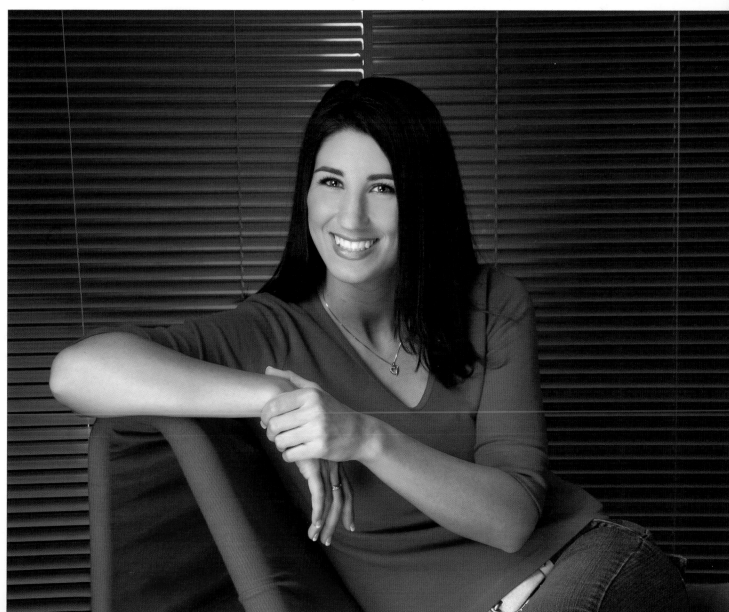

pore, and every line. Who wants to see all that? Even for many professional photographers, the only way they attempt to make reality easier on their clients' egos is to use diffusion for a softer portrait.

Maybe I'm the only one who's ever noticed, but every time I go to a seminar, the featured photographer brings out a model to demonstrate his or her theories on lighting and posing. What does this model look like? She's a goddess, right? She is perfect in every detail—tall, with the perfect shape, beautiful hair, and the perfect clothing to complete this perfect illusion of beauty.

After the lecture, you go home, all excited about the techniques you have learned and really wanting to try all these new ideas in your own studio. While you have all the knowledge from the seminar, you don't have that perfect model. So, you start experimenting with these techniques on your clients—and probably not with the same "perfect" results as the photographer at the lecture. After all, it is one thing to make "Ms. Perfect" look "perfect" in a demonstration but quite another to make Mr. and Mrs. John Q. Public look as good.

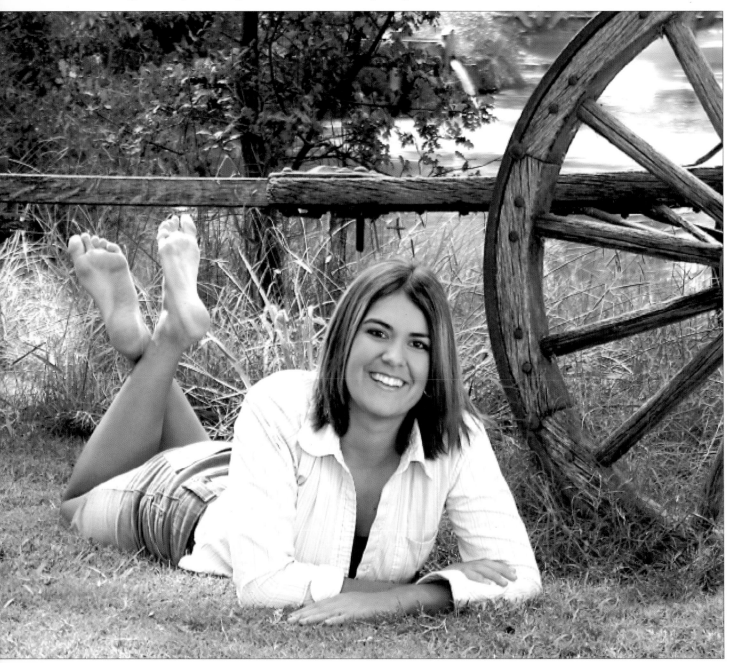

This book is for those of us who have a variety of clients, with a variety of problems, but who also want to appear beautiful.

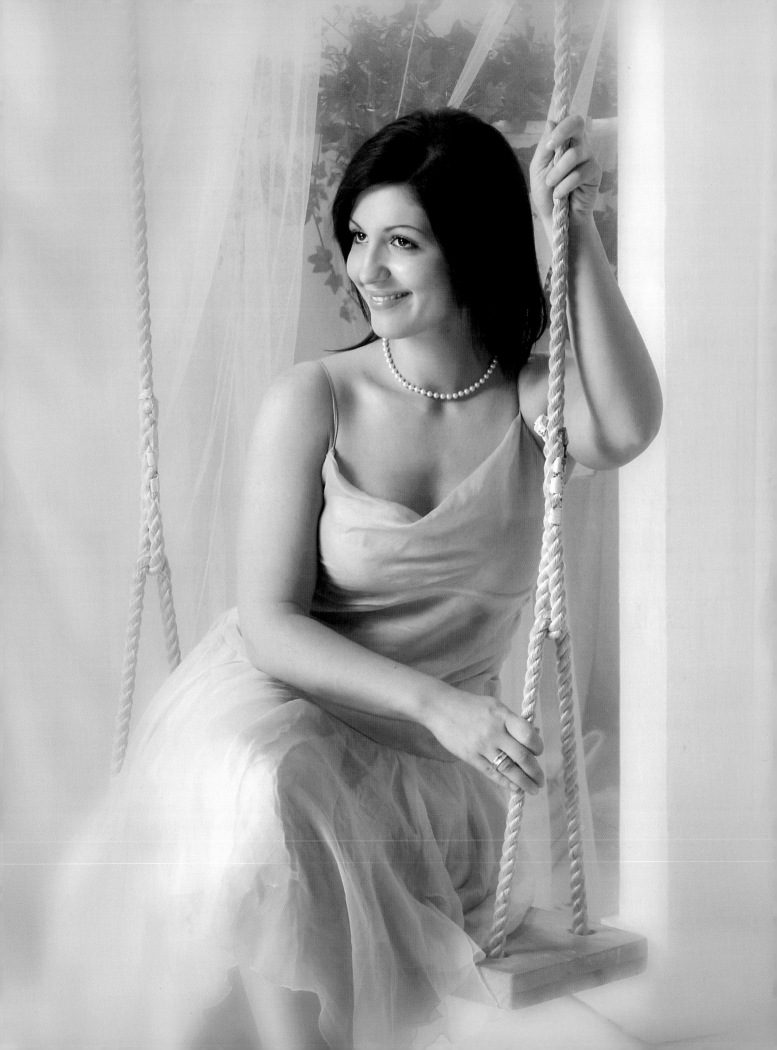

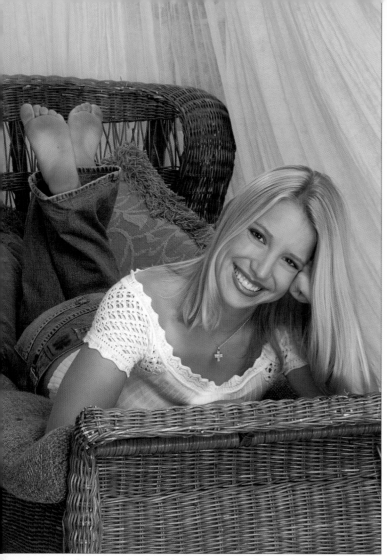 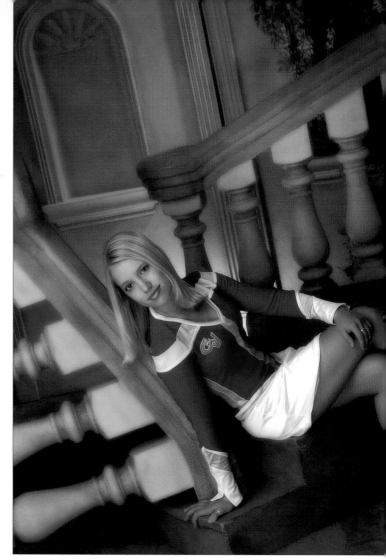

If you intend to live above the poverty line, making people look great without spending hours retouching your images is an important issue.

Yet, these are exactly the real people that we photograph every day—people who are overweight, balding, and much less photogenic than the instructor's "Ms. Perfect."

I hate to be closed minded. Maybe there actually *is* a photographer out there somewhere who makes a good living in a portrait studio that only photographs beautiful people. If there is, I would like to shake his or her hand—and then buy the studio.

This book is for all the rest of us who have a variety of clients, with a variety of problems, but who would also like to appear beautiful in their portraits. I work with high-school seniors all day long, every day of the week, and maybe 5 percent of them are attractive enough for their egos to handle looking at a portrait that shows them as they really are—a portrait that only depicts reality. Keep in mind, I'm talking about clients at an age where they have everything going for them.

They probably will never again be as thin, with as much hair and as wrinkle-free as they are at this point in their lives. As we age, the "reality" gets harder and harder to handle, but clients still want portraits that they consider flattering and attractive. Achieving that goal is the subject of this book.

We will begin by looking at ways to use lighting and posing to correct or conceal problem areas. Then we'll move on to ways to correct any remaining problems using digital technology. Considering that digital is all the rage, why, you might ask, have I decided to put off talking about it until later in the book? Well, although enhancements and corrections are easier with digital, they are still expensive—whether in terms of time or money.

So many digital photographers waste away their billable photography hours sitting in front of a computer fixing problems that should have been dealt with in the planning or photographing of the session. The "we can fix anything" way of thinking takes the profit out of your business, because whether you do the corrections yourself or pay someone else to do it, it costs you money! I consider myself a businessperson first and a photographer second. After all, if you find yourself with great images that you can't make a profit selling, you don't have a *business* you have an expensive *hobby!*

Let me explain something. An average photographer has about twenty-five billable hours per week (when you include vacations, sick days, holidays, etc.). This means that you have approximately 1300 billable hours per year. If you create $100 in sales per billable hour, your studio will generate $130,000 for the year. The average photographer, in a retail studio, gets to keep (profit) somewhere between 15 and 30 percent of the gross sales. Fifteen percent of $130,000 isn't going to keep you living at the Ritz—as a matter of fact, it will barely keep you in a cheap apartment.

In our studio, we achieve a sales averages of over $500 per hour. I can't do this by spending my time color correcting and retouching images on my computer. While you will need to be knowledgeable about digital retouching in order to set the *standards* for artwork on your photography and establish *time requirements* for these corrections, this is not work that the average photographer can afford to do personally. Instead, it can be hired out to a person making $10 an hour. If you intend to

live much above the poverty line, this is an important issue.

The good news is that, other than simple retouching for acne and other blemishes, enhancements and corrections should rarely *need* to be done if you know what you are doing when you take each portrait. Given the cost of digital work, this means you can significantly improve your efficiency and income just by being careful to identify and eliminate problems *before* you capture an image. That's exactly where we'll begin in chapter 1.

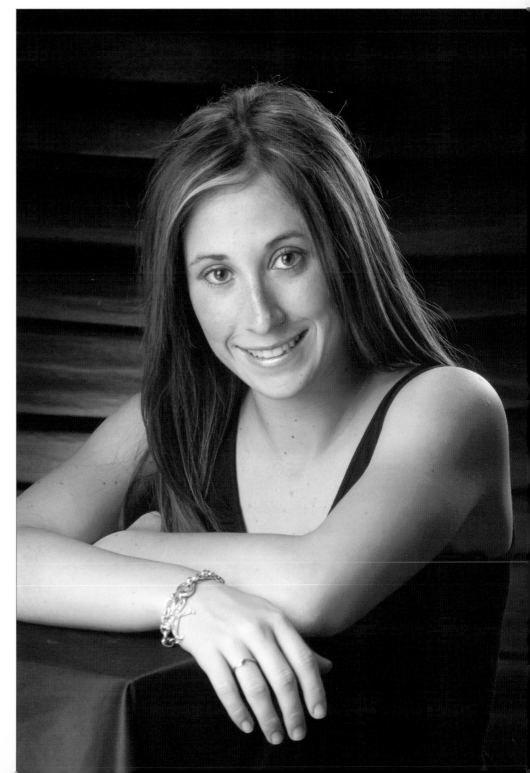

It's one thing to make "Ms. Perfect" look "perfect" in a demonstration but quite another to make Mr. and Mrs. John Q. Public look as good. Yet, these are exactly the real people that we photograph every day.

CHAPTER ONE
IDENTIFYING PROBLEMS

Almost every person has something in their appearance that they would change if they could. There are two general types of problems that you will come across when working with your clients. These are the imagined problems and the real problems.

The "imagined" problems are normally found in very attractive, very photogenic clients. Usually these problems are very slight. Most of the time the person who has these problems is the only one who can actually see them without a lot of careful searching. These problems are the hardest to correct because most photographers never take the time to speak with their clients about such issues before their session. Since no problems are readily apparent, the photographer doesn't give it a second thought. A typical imagined problem is something like, "One of my eyes is smaller than the other," "One of my ears is lower than the other," or "My smile seems crooked." As you look for this "freakish abnormality," you have to study the problem for several minutes to figure out what on earth the client is talking about.

Women are more prone to imagined problems than men, for they feel they have to live up to a higher standard. You know the double standard—a chubby guy is "stocky" while a chubby woman is "fat." A mature man has "character" while a mature woman is just "old." Many women feel that they must look like the girl on the cover of a fashion magazine, while most men feel they don't have to look any better than the guy next

door (although this is rapidly changing as guys are also becoming more and more image-conscious). This is a primary reason why I have used women for the majority of the illustrations in this book. The second reason is the fact that women generally wear clothing that is more revealing than men's clothing—meaning that any figure flaws they may have are that much more obvious.

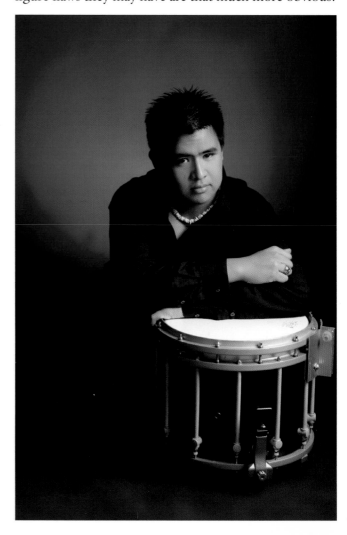

Although women are more prone to imagined appearance problems, guys are also becoming increasingly image-conscious.

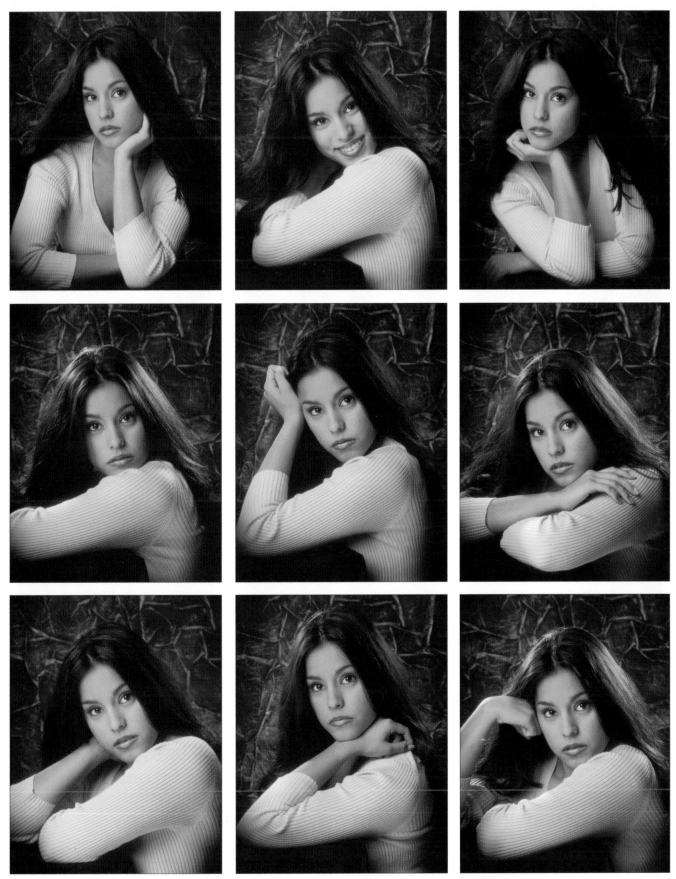

Corrective posing helps to hide the neck, a common problem area for many portrait clients.

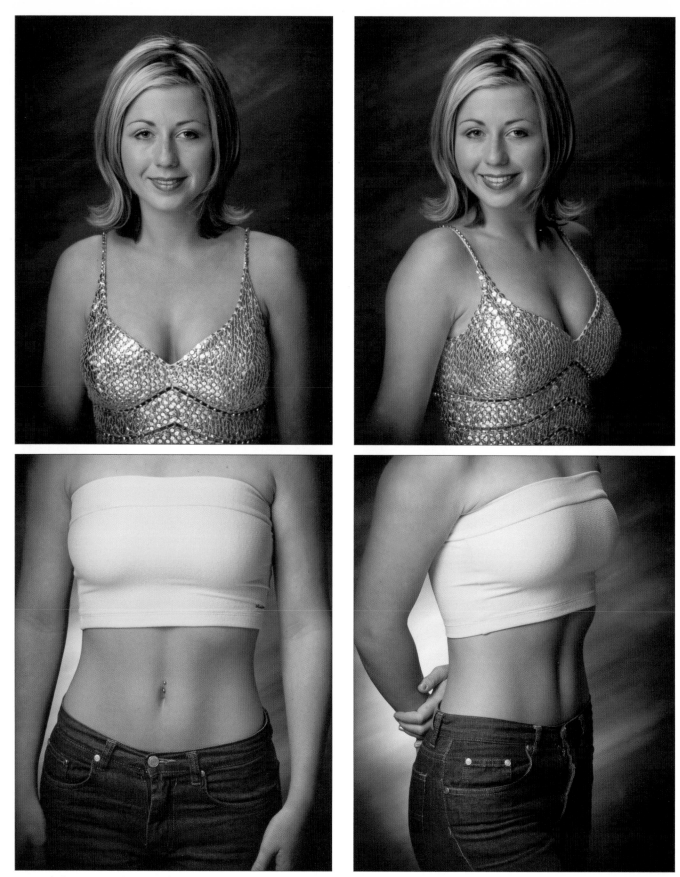

Women always want their waistlines to appear as thin as possible. Switching from a straight-on pose (left-hand images) to a pose with the body turned (right-hand images) helps to slim the waist (and also to enhance the shape of the bust).

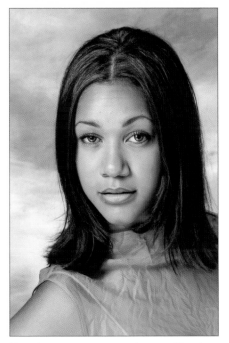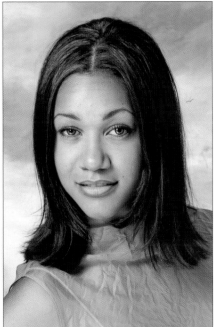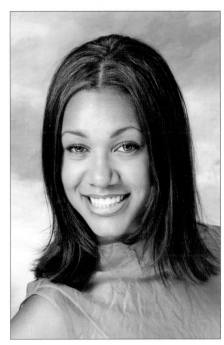

Facial expression can set the mood for the portrait. From serious and moody, to happy full smiles, work with your clients to create the best possible look for each portrait.

Guys' clothing, on the other hand, is usually loose and helps to conceal some problems.

The "real" problems are the issues that each and almost every one of us has. We are never as thin as we would like, we think our noses are too large, our ears stick out too much, and our eyes are too big or too small. These problems are easier for most photographers to correct because they are more easily identified as things that need to be disguised in the final portrait.

We may sympathize with real problems more than imagined problems, but *all* of a client's problems need to be softened in the final portraits if the session is to be profitable.

■ COMMON PROBLEMS

Neck Area. As you will notice, in many of my portraits the neck area is hidden from view. The neck area, from directly under the chin to the "Adam's apple," is the first area to show signs of weight gain and, in older clients, age. In a later section, we will discuss the many ways to hide this unsightly area in the final portraits for every type of client.

Men's Concerns. Guys want to look "buffed," not scrawny or chubby. Most guys, if they were honest (which they never are) worry about their nose being larger than they'd like, or their ears sticking out a little

too far, or both. If the guys are at all heavy, they will also be concerned with the neck area or double chin.

Women's Concerns. Ladies hate just about everything from the hairline down (just kidding—but close!). Women are not prone to large noses, but if a young lady has one you will most definitely want to minimize its appearance. Ears can usually be successfully hidden by long hair (for those who have it). Women also want to have the appearance of high cheekbones, but without looking like they have chubby cheeks or no eyes when they smile.

A woman with any kind of weight problem will worry about the thickness of her face, the neck area or double chin, as well as large shoulders, the size of her upper arms, and the size of everything else down to the bottom of her feet.

For the average-sized woman, the facial and neck areas usually are not a problem. Even thin women, though, worry about the size of their upper arms or dark hair showing on their forearms.

Most ladies with a normal bustline want their bustline to appear at least as large as it is. As the current feelings of women toward breast-enlargement surgery are generally very favorable, it is safe to say that if a woman's bustline appears slightly larger than it is in reality, it will probably be appreciated. Many times, a pose will make the bustline appear uneven, which is the worst thing you can do.

Women always want their waistlines to appear as thin as possible. If the subject has a tummy bulge, she doesn't want to see it.

In general, the only part of the uncovered leg to show in portraits is from slightly above the knee to the ankle. Of course the legs should look like they have good muscle tone and not show any signs of cellulite. Even a thin woman will usually worry about the appearance of her hips and thighs. Unless you are a woman, or are married to one, you may not realize how much women worry about this area of their bodies. It is also generally an area where extra weight is very apparent.

Some women love their feet, others hate them. About ten years ago, we started photographing seniors barefoot when the clothing and sets were appropriate. The idea caught on and became very popular with young ladies who usually spend a lot of time putting polish on their toenails. We quickly learned, however, how much *some* women hate their feet—when we asked them to remove their shoes, we'd see a look of total horror. Based on their reaction, I expected to see feet with seven toes!

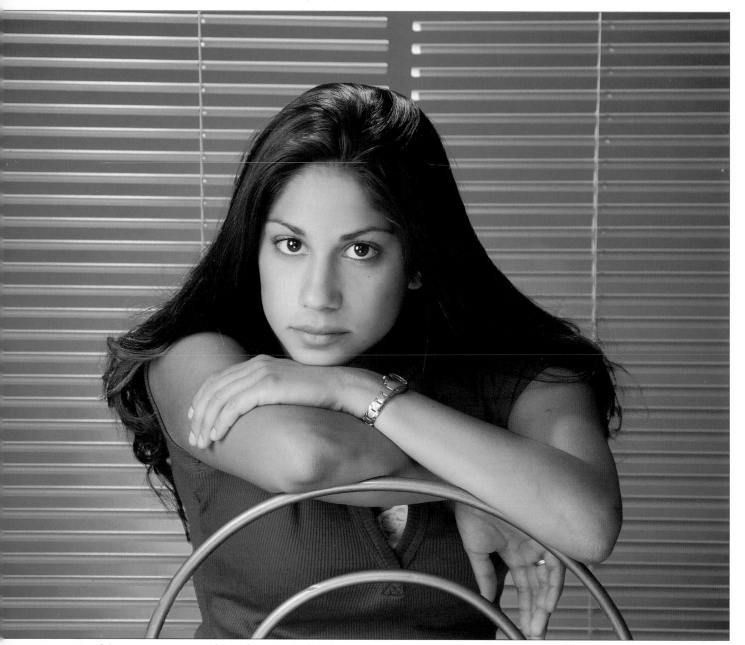

Careful posing can minimize (above) or enhance (facing page) the bustline.

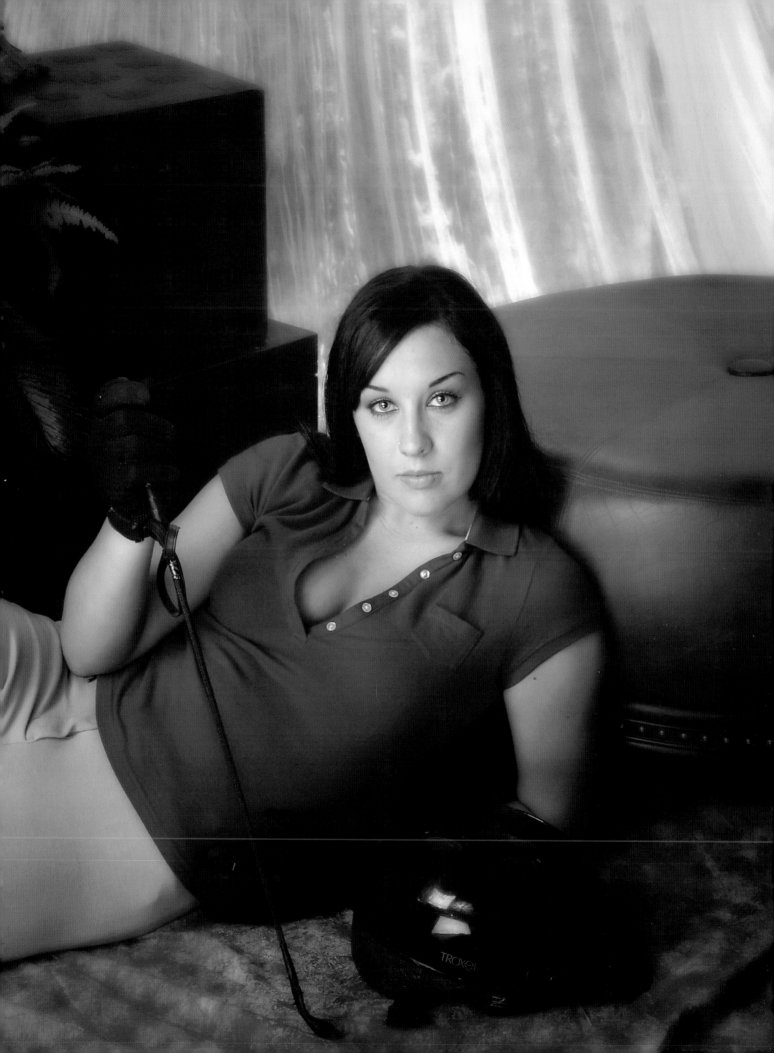

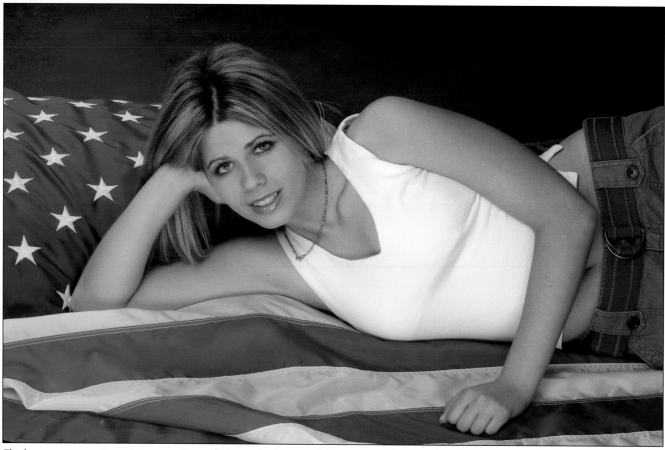

The longer you practice using corrective techniques, the faster and better you will get at identifying problems and developing solutions.

■ QUICKLY EVALUATING A CLIENT'S PROBLEMS

Summing up the problems a client has can be accomplished in a matter of seconds. When you sit someone down with the main light turned on, you can immediately start to see what that person's strengths and weaknesses are. You can see how wide the face is, how well the subject's eyes reflect light, and identify flaws like unevenly sized eyes, large noses, or prominent ears that need to be hidden.

As you sum up the problems that need to be addressed, you can start to make decisions about what side of the subject the main light should be placed on, what poses you can use to hide this individual's flaws, which of the client's outfits would give you the most to work with (in terms of disguising the problems the client has), if the person should do full-length images or not, or if they have long enough hair to hide the shoulders and arms so the client may wear sleeveless tops.

The longer you practice using corrective techniques, the faster and better you will get at identifying problems and developing workable solutions. It's just like when you started into photography. You would photograph someone, and when the proofs came back you would find that the subject's feet weren't right, that their hands looked funny, or that their clothing wasn't laying properly. In time, you learned to "scan" the subject quickly from head to toe and identify anything in the pose or clothing that wasn't right. The same is true for finding and correcting client's problems; with some practice, it just takes a few seconds.

CHAPTER TWO

WORKING WITH CLIENTS

As photographers, we worry constantly about improving our lighting, our posing, and even our marketing plans, but often we completely overlook the most important part of our businesses—our clients. If you think, as many photographers do, that you know more about what your client should have than your client does, your client will prove you wrong every time.

You may be the creator of "your art," but the client is the one who must live with your creation and, in the end, is the one who determines whether a portrait is "art" or not.

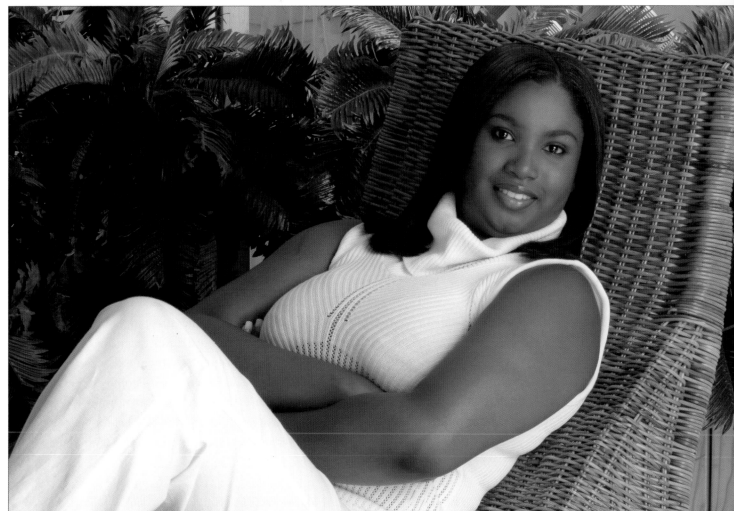

After working with seniors for eighteen years, I pretty much know the areas of the face and body that the average seventeen-year-old man or woman worries about the most.

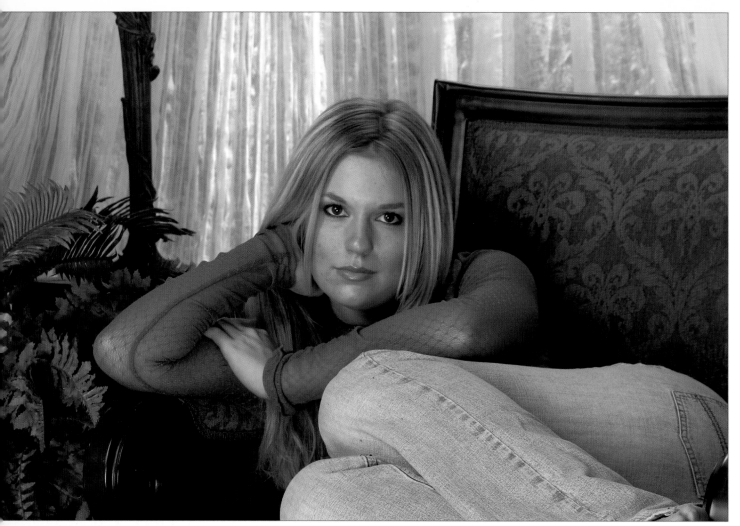

Before you create a portrait for a client (a portrait that you actually want the client to purchase), you had better figure out what that client expects his or her portrait to look like.

We are very conscious to deliver to our clients the products they want. We talk with them as much as possible. We ask questions, give the clients questionnaires, and try to make the exchange of ideas (and any discussion of problem features, real or imagined) as easy as humanly possible. Still, most clients will not come right out and tell you what they consider to be problems with their appearance. They won't write it down on a questionnaire. The majority of the time, the mothers of the seniors are the ones who alert us to issues with their sons' or daughters' appearances—and even this doesn't happen as often as we would like.

To practice corrective lighting and posing in your studio, you have to learn about human nature. Most of us worry about the same things. We are not as different as most people think. After working with seniors for eighteen years, I pretty much know the areas of the face and body that the average seventeen-year-old man or woman worries about the most.

■ COMMUNICATION SKILLS

Before you create a portrait for a client (a portrait that you actually want the client to purchase), you had better figure out what that client expects his or her portrait to look like. As you talk with your client, you must be sensitive to his or her feelings. People are embarrassed by the flaws they have. As a professional, you must make it easy for them to tell you what the problems are.

This will be easier if you educate your clients from the beginning. Let them know that everybody has things in their appearance that they would change if they could. Explain that if you know what the client's concerns are, you can easily correct many problems in their portraits. In the materials we provide to seniors before the session, we carefully explain that, although we can correct problems in someone's appearance (like weight, double chins, or large noses), we cannot correct the problems that arise from not planning their session properly.

It is also important to define what problems you can fix. Some clients will assume that your studio will take care of *all* their problems. When they come in with wrinkled clothing, unwashed hair, and thick glasses (with the glass still in the frame) they will say, "Well, you said you would fix all the problems in my appearance!" We go over what can be corrected in the lighting and posing, what digital retouching can correct, and what retouching costs them in the event that they don't want to take the time to prepare for their session properly.

In business, almost every problem that arises comes from a lack of communication. In a portrait studio, most problems stem from clients not understanding their responsibilities for the outcome of their session, or the photographer not knowing what the expectations of his or her client were.

■ MAKING YOUR CLIENTS FEEL COMFORTABLE

There are many ways to get a client to tell you if there is a problem without making them feeling embarrassed or awkward. Before we start the session, we ask questions to which the client only has to answer "yes" or "no"—and we phrase them to make it clear that lots of other people worry about the particular issue we're discussing.

In a portrait studio, most problems stem from clients not understanding their responsibilities for the outcome of their session, or the photographer not knowing what the expectations of his or her client were.

For example, a typical situation occurs when senior girls bring in sleeveless tops (something we specifically recommend against in our consultation materials). The minute I see them, I explain, "Sleeveless tops are fine." This doesn't make the senior feel like an idiot for not following the guidelines.

Then I continue, "The only problem is that a lot of ladies worry about their upper arms looking large or hair showing on the forearms. Does that bother you?" Either she will smile and say "Yes" or she will say "No." By phrasing your question carefully, you can make it

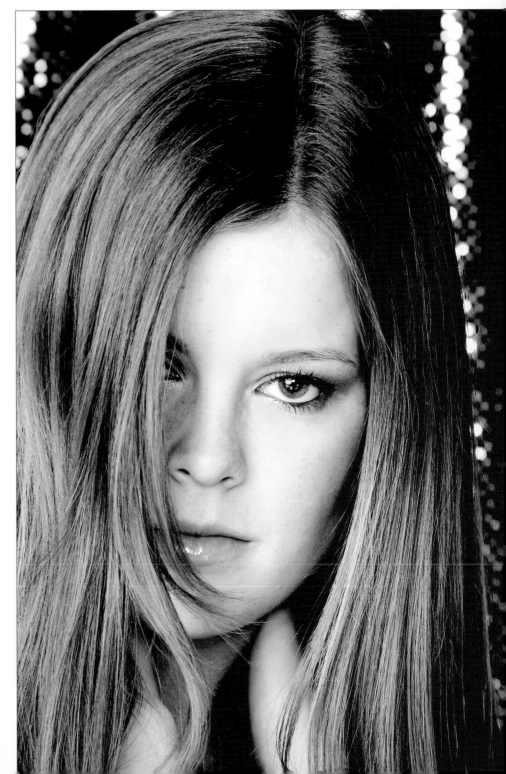

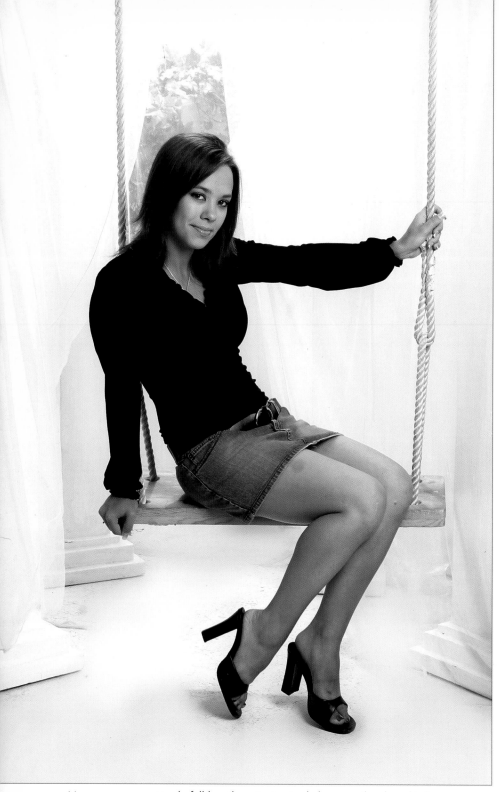

Many women want to do full-length portraits simply because they bought shoes to coordinate with their outfit.

casual photograph like we are doing it looks cute to go barefoot. If you don't mind, you can come out of the dressing room barefoot, but if you'd rather not go barefoot, you can keep your shoes on." When the girl comes out of the dressing room, not a word needs to be said.

The hardest spot to be in occurs when a client wants to do a pose that you know she or he should avoid. For instance, a really heavy girl selects a pose from the sample books of a thin girl in a very striking pose. What do you do? There is only so much that corrective lighting and posing can do. No matter how you pose or light a girl who is very overweight, in a full-length pose she will not appear thin enough to be acceptable to her. In a case like this, you must advise the client to do head-and-shoulders poses.

Situations like this happen more often than most people think. To sympathize with these clients, you must understand why this happens. When I first started in photography, I would think to myself, "Hey, that girl has arms like a tree trunk and she brings in nothing but sleeveless tops—what an idiot!" Back then, I resented these clients because I felt that they made my job harder. What I didn't understand is the way human eyes and brains work to save our egos from having to handle reality when we look in the mirror. You might gain ten or twenty pounds and lose some hair, yet it's not until you see yourself in a picture that you really notice these changes. You think to yourself, "I look in the mirror every day. Where has this fat, old, hairless guy been hiding?"

Fortunately, it is not so much *what* you say to clients that is important, rather it is the *way* you say it.

easy for them to voice their concerns without being embarrassed.

The best way to handle a possibly embarrassing situations is to give the client two options, so no answer is needed. We do this with the "barefoot" issue. Rather than ask if a girl hates her feet, we explain: "With a

For every problem and potentially embarrassing situation there is a way to handle it without making yourself look unprofessional or seeing your client turn red.

For example, when I see a heavier girl with a lot of boxes of shoes, I know I am going to have a problem and I need to say something the minute I show her into the dressing room. I first explain, "Many ladies go on a shopping spree to buy a matching pair of shoes for every outfit. Since they bought them, they want them to show in their portraits. The problem is that when you order your wallets for family and friends, the full-length poses make it very hard to really see your face that well." (This gets the girl to accept that not all the poses should be done full-length.)

Then I continue, "Most women worry about looking as thin as possible. The areas that women worry about the most are their hips and thighs. This is why most of the portraits are done from the waist up, not to show this area." Next I ask, "Now, are there any outfits that you want to take full-length, or do you want to do everything from the waist up?" She will usually think for a second and say she wants everything from the waist up. This avoids telling her she can't take full-lengths, or being brutally honest and telling her she shouldn't take them.

Should the girl be really attached to her shoes and not follow what I am trying to tell her, I go to the parent or friend she is with and explain that if we do the portraits full-length, I worry that she won't like them, because women worry so much about looking thin. Once I explain this to the mother, she can tell her daughter not to do full-lengths, or a friend can help enlighten her without causing embarrassment.

■ REALLY LISTENING

Everyone has a feature or aspect of their appearance that they are self-conscious about. Some of these problems are so slight you might not even see them, but that is irrelevant. The client will see them, and the client is the one paying the bill for the portraits you create.

Often, photographers forget this. I was once at an outdoor location that is used by several other local photographers. As I was waiting for my client to change her clothing, I had nothing better to do than listen to another photographer working with his own client. The

In most cases, it's extremely easy to photograph a variety of views of the client—from close-ups to full-length portraits. This is a good way to ensure that everyone will find something they like when ordering images from the session.

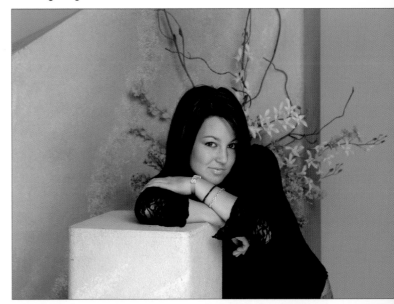

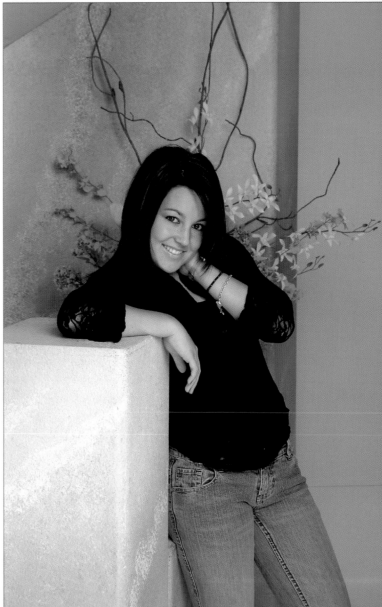

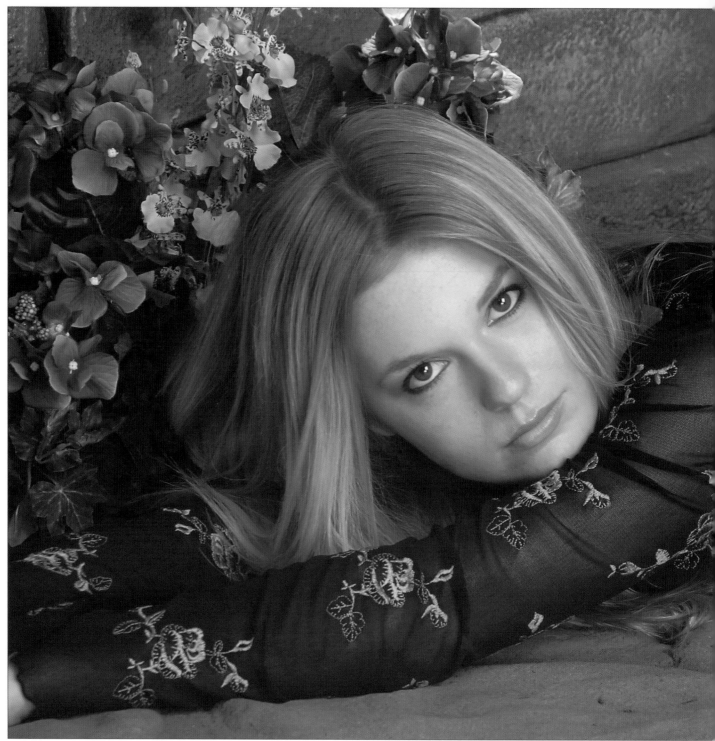

subject was a young woman, a few years out of high school. The photographer instructed his client to hop up on a rock that was near the pond. As the woman sat down, her pant leg inched up, revealing her white socks gleaming out of her dark-blue denim pant leg. She asked, "Are my white socks going to show?" The photographer, who was obviously about as compassionate as he was educated in customer service, quickly re-sponded, "Hey, if you didn't want them to show, you shouldn't have worn them!" He then proceeded to take the portrait full-length, showing the white socks.

How hard would it have been to compose the portrait as a close-up or three-quarter-length, or have the woman take off her shoes and go barefoot? Instead, this photographer refused to try something outside of what he had always done. That was probably his favorite

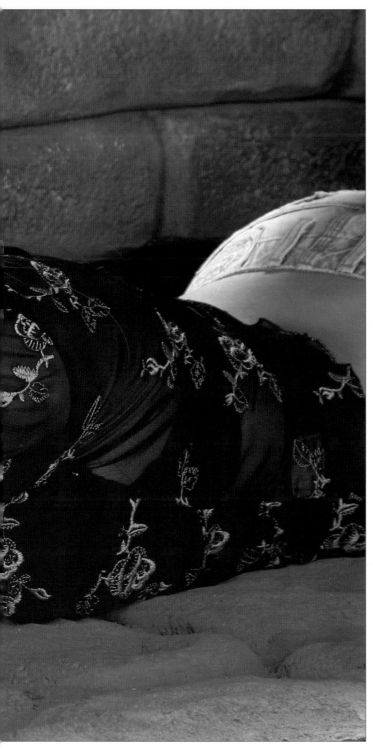

If you want to live very far above the poverty line, you had better take every problem seriously and make sure your client doesn't see areas of concern in his or her final portraits.

funny. That's okay, but if you want to live very far above the poverty line, you had better take these problems seriously and make sure that your client doesn't see them in his or her final portraits.

■ TACT

Photographers don't usually spend a lot of time thinking about how to talk with their clients without offending them. While watching photographers work with clients, I have heard instructions like, "Sit your butt here," "Stick out your chest," "Suck it in just before I take the picture, so your belly doesn't show as much," "Look sexy at the camera," and "Show me a little leg"! I am sure the women who were instructed in this way didn't feel very comfortable with or confident about their chosen photographers.

Whether you are discussing a client's problems or directing them into poses, there are certain words that are unprofessional to use in reference to your clients' bodies. In place of "butt," choose "bottom" or "seat." Never say "crotch," just tell the client to turn his or her legs in one direction or another so that this area isn't a problem. Instead of "Stick out your chest," say "Arch your back." Replace "Suck in your stomach" with an instruction to "Breath in just before I take the portrait." To direct a client for a "sexy look," simply have the subject make direct eye contact with the camera, lower her chin, and breath through her lips so there is slight separation between them.

No matter how clinical you are when you talk about a woman's breasts, if you are of the opposite sex, you will embarrass them. The only time it is necessary to discuss that part of the anatomy is when the pose makes the woman's breasts appear uneven. When this situation comes up, I just explain to the client how to move in order to fix the problem, without telling the client exactly what problem we are fixing. Once in a while, we have a young lady show up for a session wearing a top or dress that is really low cut. In this situation, you need to find an alternative for your client. If there is way too much of your client showing, you may explain that this dress is a little "low cut" for the type of portraits she is taking.

rock, and he took every portrait at "his rock" and as a full-length—or he just didn't take it. In our profession, the saying "Ours is not to ask why" certainly applies. Our job is simply to fix it. A client's problems may seem insignificant to you—you may even think they are

CHAPTER THREE
CORRECTIVE LIGHTING

Because of our training, most photographers might think that corrective lighting would do the most to hide flaws. Well, it doesn't! In fact, it is our "training" in how to light a portrait that is the biggest problem. When we start to learn about lighting, we learn that light is said to be our "paint brush." Corrective lighting, however, actually relies on shadow, not light.

Any student photographer with two lights and a meter can create a decent portrait—just put the main light at a 45-degree angle to the subject and place the other light behind the camera. Set the lights so the main light is two stops brighter than the light behind the camera, stick a diffusion filter on the lens, and there you have it—I have just taught everyone with any knowledge of photography to create a realistic portrait with the appearance of a third dimension. This is the lighting setup mall studios use because it is easy to learn, easy to use and, for most of the buying public, acceptable for a cheap portrait. Unfortunately, this is also the lighting setup that many *professional* studios use. While clients will accept this type of portrait if they are getting it cheap, they are not going to pay a professional studio's price for something they could get at the mall for much less. Professionals need to deliver more

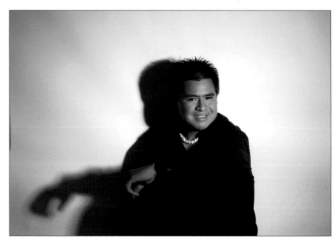

It is shadow that gives a portrait dimension, and it is shadow that lets you disguise your clients' flaws.

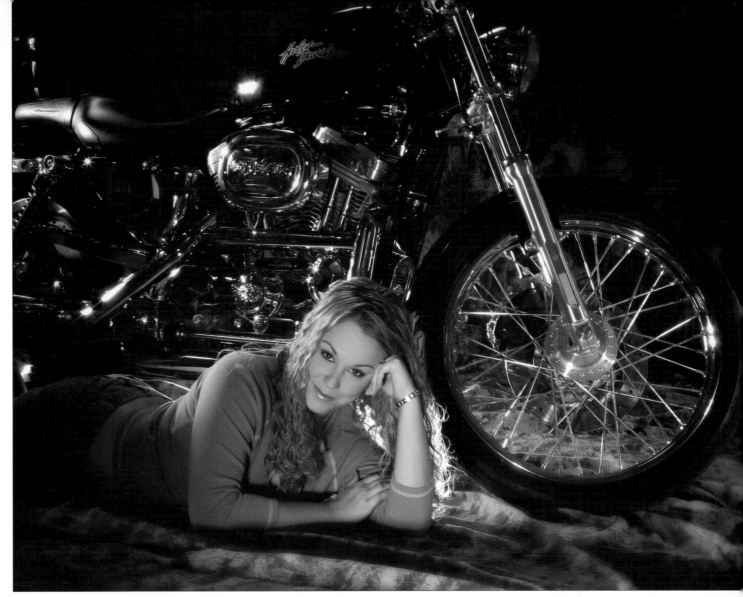

Shooting in a dark area ensures that no light is bounced off the walls or items in the room, so I can put light and shadow exactly where I want it and not have it diminished by the surroundings.

than an "acceptable" portrait. This is where shadow comes in.

It's obvious that not much would exist in an image without light, but it is the darkness that draws the viewer's eye to the light. It is shadow that gives a portrait dimension, and it is shadow that lets you disguise your clients' flaws—flaws they aren't paying to see (or, perhaps better, flaws they won't pay for if they do see them).

Corrective lighting is about control of light, but even more importantly, it is about control of shadow. In a basic lighting setup like I described earlier, control is impossible. Combine a large main light and a fill light with the white walls of most studios and you have light bouncing around off of everything. The three pitfalls of the average lighting setup are:

1. **Using a main light modifier that is too large and uncontrollable.** Because of our love of light, we reason that bigger is better. In fact, the larger your light source/modifier, the less control you have. If you use umbrellas and want to control your light better, throw them away and buy a small softbox with louvers.

2. **Using fill flash instead of reflector fill.** The fewer lights you can use in your camera room, the more control over the lighting you will have. When you use fill flash, you get fill everywhere and have no control of the shadow formation in specific areas.

3. **Using light-colored camera rooms.** These add to the lack of control in the shadow areas. In corrective lighting, I want light to fall only and pre-

cisely where I put it. That can't happen with white or cream-colored walls and floors. These light-colored surfaces themselves become a source of fill light, just like using a white reflector.

■ CAMERA AREA

Although my studio features several camera areas, it's the low-key area where we use corrective lighting. In this area, we've worked to eliminate features that reduce the control you have over your lighting. Thus, the entire area is black—walls, floor, etc. Even the props and furniture are all black, or least very dark. This ensures that no light is bounced off the walls or items in the room, so I can put light and shadow exactly where I want it and not have it diminished by the surroundings.

■ THE LIGHTS

The Main Light. The main light that we use with corrective lighting is a 24x36-inch softbox with a recessed front panel and louvers. This allows us to put light precisely where it is wanted, without it spilling into areas where it isn't. The size of the box allows us to get a softer light when the box is placed close to the subject, but we can make the light more contrasty by pulling it back just a little.

There are some differences to be aware of when working with smaller light sources that produce more contrasty light. First, you have to watch out for shadows in unwanted places—you can get some harsh shadows on the unlit side of the nose, for example. Second, small light sources can't be feathered like large ones. With large light sources that don't have a recessed front, you can use just the edge of the light to soften the light or cut down on the output. If you try that with a small louvered box, you will have light falloff on

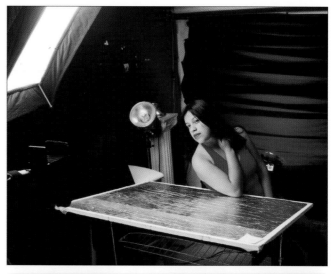

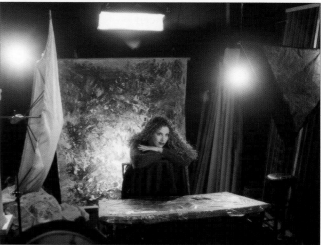

We use a heavy-duty drafting table covered with thin mylar as a posing table and reflector (top). In our low-key camera area, everything is dark to ensure that light won't bounce around (above).

the highlight side of the face. The light from this type of box goes precisely where you put it and nowhere else.

The louvers on the main light control the light from side to side. They eliminate light rays from spilling out of the side of the box. To control light from the top and bottom of the box, you must either feather the

---

CONCEAL THE FLAWS BUT LIGHT FOR THE SUBJECT

Of course, you can't light a subject just to correct flaws. Consider how you'd shoot a portrait of a subject in glasses. This is an excellent example of lighting to correct the flaw (glass glare) rather than to make the client look good. Of the many ways I have seen and tried to eliminate the glare in glasses, I have never seen one that doesn't make the lighting on the subject's face suffer. As a professional, you have to know when to use correction and when to inform your client of his or her responsibilities for the outcome of the session. In this case, empty frames or nonglare lenses are the only way to ensure a pleasing portrait that is taken to make your client look their best.

light or use a gobo to block the light from hitting areas that you want to keep in shadow.

The Fill Light. To add fill light only where it is wanted, we use a reflector. For any of you fans of using a flash to fill the shadow, you are about to be offended. I (like all young photographers) was taught that you use a flash to fill the shadow. You put this enormous light source at the back wall of the camera room, and it literally fills your entire camera room to a certain level of light. I was then instructed, as most of you were, that to avoid flat lighting you would use a ratio between the main light and fill of 3:1 without diffusion, and 4:1 with diffusion.

I worked with this for quite some time. It wasn't until a young African-American woman came into my studio and talked with me about doing her portraits that I saw a problem. She asked me if I had ever photographed an African-American person before. I thought for a minute and realized that I never had. She explained that she had had her portraits taken several times, at several places, and they just didn't look right.

She said they had very heavy shadows. When she said this, I suddenly realized how limiting the use of fill flash was. My first thought was, "Wait a minute, I use a 3:1 or 4:1 ratio, but that is for a light skin tone. What ratio do I use for all the other shades of skin?"

Well, I did the session, but I did it with a reflector for fill, so I could see on her face, with her skin tone and facial structure, how much shadow or fill I wanted. She loved the portraits, and I learned a major lesson. You can know what the ratio of lighting is by metering, but when you use a flash fill you will never know what the "perfect" ratio of light is for each individual's skin tone and facial structure.

In this country we have such a variety of people, with different shades of skin, different facial structures, and (need I point out?) different problems and flaws to hide. The only way to evaluate the right amount of fill is to see it with your own eyes.

If you don't believe that skin tone makes a difference, photograph three people with the exact same light on them and the background. Select one person

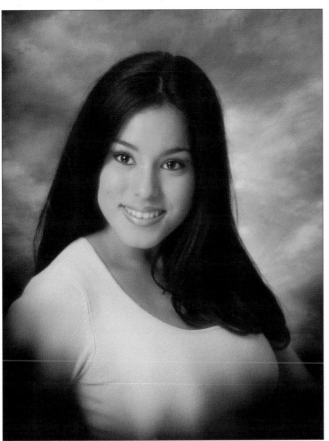 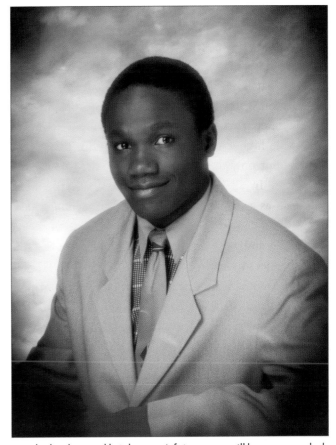

With identical lighting, the skin tone of the subject can make a difference in the background brightness. A fair person will have a very dark background (left) and a person with a dark complexion will have a very bright background (right).

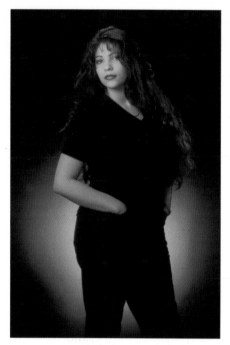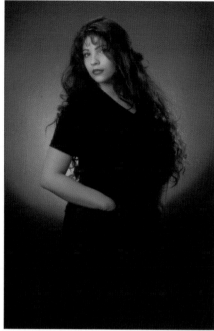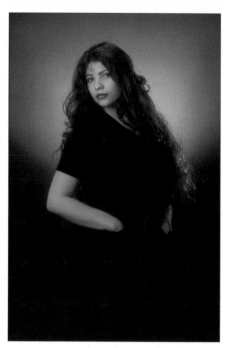

Use separation light to accent only the parts of the client you want to draw attention to. Three variations are shown here, with separation light on the lower body (left), upper body (center), and head and shoulders (right).

who is very fair, one with an olive complexion or a great suntan, and one person with a very dark complexion. You will quickly see the difference in the backgrounds. Because of the way the different skin tones are printed, the very fair person will have a very dark background, the olive-skinned or suntanned person will have a background that is normal, and the person with the dark complexion will have a very bright background.

The Separation Light. Because corrective lighting relies on a higher contrast lighting, you must use separation—but only in the areas of your client you *want* separated. In all portraits, we use a small strip light overhead as a hair light. Since this light is aimed back toward the camera, it meters one stop less than the main light and yet provides a soft highlight on the top of the subject's hair and shoulders.

For clients with long hair, we use two lights behind the subject. Each is placed at a 45-degree angle to the subject. These lights are set to meter at the same reading as the main light for blond hair or lighter clothing, or to one stop more than the main light reading for black hair and clothing. These accent lights are also fitted with barndoors to keep the light from hitting an area of the subject we don't want to illuminate.

The idea is that you don't want to see a perfect outline of the body in a problem area. For very heavy people, you don't want to see an outline of the body at all. With the background light low and the subject standing in dark clothes against a dark background, you separate the hips and thighs (the same hips and thighs you know your client will worry about looking large). Raising the background light to waist height will separate the waistline and chest, making them more noticeable. Elevate the separation light to the height of the shoulders, and only the head and shoulders will be separated, leaving the body to blend with the background.

The greater the intensity of the background light, the more attention it draws to whatever part of the body it is separating—unless the subject is wearing lighter-colored clothing. Often a client will select a dark background and want to wear lighter-colored clothing with it. In this situation, by increasing the background light to match the brighter tone of the outfit, you will actually lessen the attention drawn to this area. By co-ordinating the tone of the clothes and the background (whether dark on dark or light on light), you can bring the focus of the portrait away from the person's body and to his or her face. If, on the other hand, you create contrast between the clothing and background, you will attract attention to the subject's body.

Whenever weight is an issue and the subject has long hair, we leave the background as dark as possible and put a light directly behind the subject, facing toward the camera, to give the hair an intense rim light all around the edges. This draws the attention directly to the facial area and keeps the viewer's eye away from the shoulders, arms, and upper body.

■ POSITIONING THE LIGHTS

The angle of the main light is always determined by the orientation of the subject's nose. With the subject's nose pointed directly at the camera, the main light should be at approximately a 45-degree angle to the camera. To add shadow or bring out more facial structure, you may increase the angle of the light, but this is the angle at which most portraits will be taken. The great thing is that the light always stays at approximately a 45-degree angle to where the nose is pointing—even when you go to a profile.

Once the main light is in position, you have to decide how much of the shadow area needs to be filled.

With a reflector as a fill, what you see is what you get. Start with no fill at all. If the portrait looks great, don't add any fill. Somewhere along the line, you were probably told (like I was) that you have to see some detail in the shadow area. Wrong! If a shadow that goes black is what makes your subject look his best, then that is the perfect lighting to use on that individual client.

Most of the time, however, some fill is necessary to bring the shadows to a printable level. Start with the reflector far away from the subject, then move it progressively closer until you get the effect you want. Whether you use a white or soft silver reflector will ultimately depend on what you have on hand. I use a soft silver one and pull it out farther than I would have to with a white reflector.

With the main light and fill reflector in place, separating the subject from the background becomes the next step. Again, there are no rules. You have one objective, and that is to make your client look as good

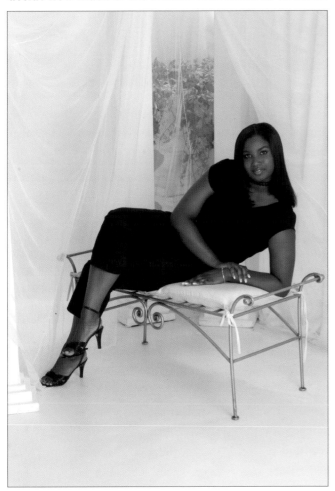
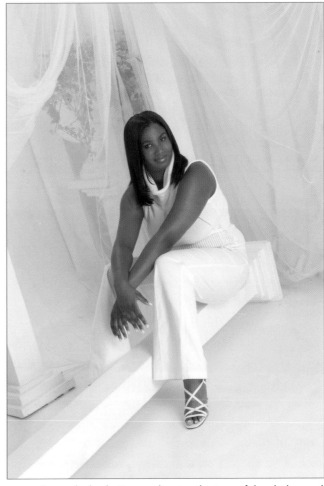

Creating contrast between the clothing and the background (left) draws attention to the body. By coordinating the tone of the clothes and the background (right), you can bring the focus of the portrait away from the person's body and to his or her face.

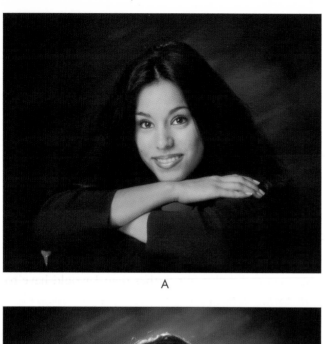

A

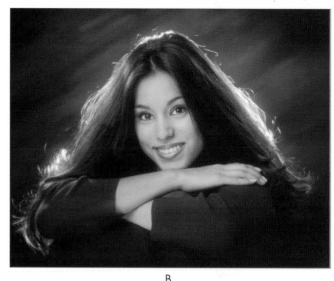

B

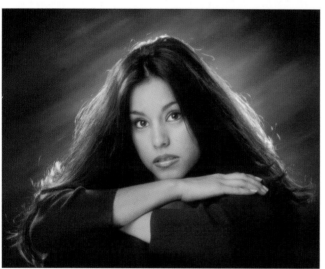

C

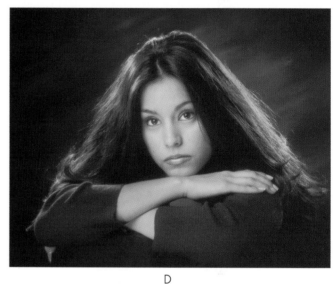

D

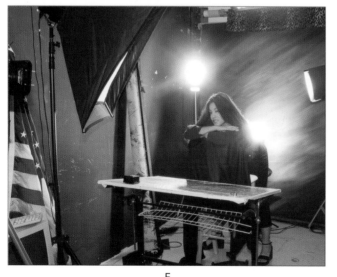

E

The number-one complaint from clients with dark hair is that, in many previous portraits, they seemed to blend into the background (A). With clients who have hair (not bald), we typically use a strip light overhead to add soft separation to the head and shoulders. For someone with long hair, we add two accent lights with barndoors at a 45-degree angle, and a final light is placed directly behind the subject's head. This light is angled back through the hair toward the camera (we call it a halo light). This can cause stray hairs to become very visible (B). In Image C, the appearance of stray hairs has been minimized by reducing the intensity of the halo light. Sometimes this isn't enough, and we eliminate the halo light (D). An overview of the setup is shown in image E.

as possible. Remember, no background or separation from the background means no point of reference behind the subject. No point of reference behind or in front of your subject means no depth in the portrait.

We begin with the hair. For this, a strip light attached to the ceiling gives a soft separation to the hair and shoulders when the light is metered at one stop less than the main light. To finish the separation, we add a light aimed directly toward the hair behind the subject. This creates an intense rim light all the way around the hair. This meters from one stop more than the main light for blond hair to three stops more than the main for brunette or black hair.

This type of portrait is simple, but vary salable, for it gives any client a version of reality they can live with.

■ LIGHTING THE FULL-LENGTH POSE

Since senior portraits became a hot topic in the early 1980s, lecturers, authors, and educators have hailed the offering of full-length portraits as one of the best ways to set your studio apart from the contracted studios. I feel that the full- or three-quarter-length pose has been oversimplified and its importance overstated. Once again, I have never seen one of those photographer/ lecturers stroll out with a model who is five-feet tall with a tummy bulge and short legs. Therefore, the first rule of full- or three-quarter-length poses is that if there is any reason not to do them, then don't. (Laziness doesn't qualify as a valid reason not to do a full-length pose, however.) Using corrective lighting, selecting the proper background and making good clothing choices can do a lot to enhance a person's appearance, but if the subject has significant problems (significant weight issues, large scars from burns, etc.) no amount of enhancements can produce a salable portrait in a full-length pose.

Low-Key Setups. Corrective lighting for a full- or three-quarter-length pose relies heavily on using light's falloff to act as a vignette, thereby throwing certain problem areas into complete darkness and not allowing the camera to record the problems or flaws in those areas. The second lighting tool for correction is one we

In high-key portraiture, correction relies on the clothing selection, set, and pose.

have already discussed—separation. By selecting the area of the body you wish to separate from the background, you determine which area of the body the viewer's eye will be drawn to.

A 24x36-inch louvered softbox may not be the first main-light choice for the classic full-length portrait, but it is perfect for beautifully lighting the facial area and letting the rest of the subject fall completely into shadow. With this accomplished, you can proceed to add separation to the areas of the subject you feel should be seen in the portrait. This is no different for thinning a waistline than for concealing a balding head. You only separate the subject in an area that the client would want to see.

High-Key Setups. When you move to high key, lighting can do very little. In high-key portraiture, correction relies on the clothing selection, set, and pose. For this type of image, we use large light sources, then employ the other elements of the scene to hide the

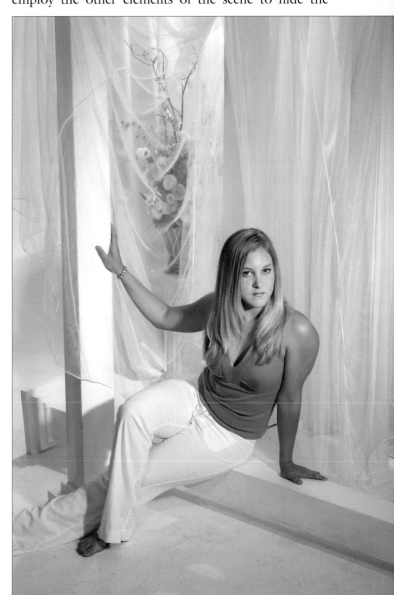

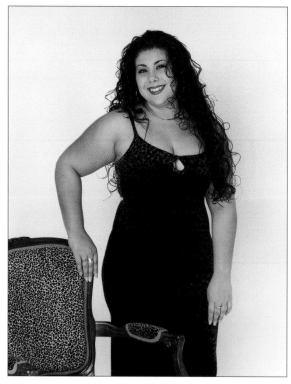

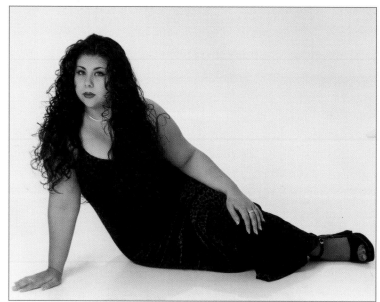

When the client's clothes contrast strongly with the background, it calls attention to the shape of the body (left). Careful corrective posing can still help to create a flattering portrait (above).

client's flaws. Often, something as simple as a good pose and a client's long hair can be enough to make the subject happy with the way she looks.

While very popular, high-key images are best avoided by anyone with a weight problem. With the softer, less contrasty look, faces appear heavier and bodies wider. We have actually had many thin clients notice the difference between how wide their faces look on the high-key backgrounds as opposed to the low-key setup.

■ GRID SPOTS

In high-school senior photography, the use of spotlights has been popular for many years, especially for portraits in black & white. The hard, contrasty lighting produces a very theatrical feeling. Spotlights also have the ability to focus the viewer's eye precisely where you want it to go. When used as a main light, the beam of the spot leads the eye to the facial area, while letting the rest of the body fall into shadow.

Often, we simply use a single grid spot as the entire lighting for the portrait. A very popular idea for seniors is to set the subject up against a white wall and let the heavy shadow of the subject projected on the wall provide a dramatic background. Watch out for the creation of deep shadows on the face when doing this. While dark shadows look good in the background, heavy shadows on the face can be quite unsightly. The easiest way to handle this is to turn the face more into the spotlight and work with the spot at no more than a 45-degree angle from the camera. Using the spot in this way gives you the greatest contrast and the most options for hiding flaws.

We also use grids as accent lights, working with the main light to draw attention to the face. Simply put the

DON'T CREATE NEW FLAWS BY CORRECTING EXISTING ONES

When considering how to light a portrait to correct flaws, you have to remember that by correcting one flaw, you can actually make another flaw more apparent. A good example would be a person with a wide face and a very large nose. You can thin the face by increasing the contrast of the lighting and creating a larger shadow area, but if you are not careful, you can also create more shadows on the side of the nose, drawing more attention to its size. The same thing can happen with a person with bad skin. The more contrasty the light, the more the skin's imperfections become visible (of course, this can be eliminated in retouching).

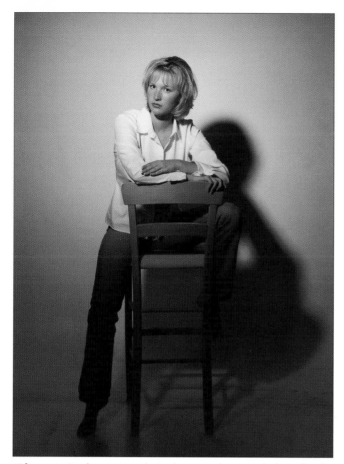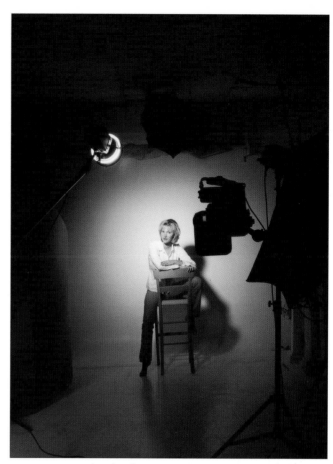

Often, we simply use a single grid spot as the entire lighting for the portrait. A very popular idea for seniors is to set the subject up against a white wall and let the heavy shadow of the subject projected on the wall provide a dramatic background.

sphere of light on the facial area after your normal lighting is in place. The spot should be set one-half to one stop more than the main light, depending on how noticeable you want the light from the spot to appear. This little bit of light helps smooth the complexion, but more important is the effect it has on the color of the eyes. If you can see any color around the pupil, this accent light makes it much more vibrant. Anytime I see someone come in who has colored contacts or color around the pupils of their eyes, I do at least one of their poses with this accent light.

No matter how you use grid spots, they give you the ability to offer your client different styles of lighting that create different styles of portraits. A photographer who can only offer his clients one style of lighting and one style of portraits can only appeal to one type of client with one type of taste.

CHAPTER FOUR

CORRECTIVE POSING

Posing is the most exciting part of what we as professional photographers do. A pose can make even the most basic type of portrait come alive. Other than the expression, nothing will sell more than the pose. Posing can also do more to hide clients' flaws than any other method of eliminating problems—and probably as much as all of the others combined. Posing alone can hide almost every flaw that the human body can have. For every person, in every outfit, there is a pose that can make them look great. You just have to find it. This leads us to the first part of corrective posing, namely, finding interesting poses to offer your clients. The second part of corrective posing is to convert the poses you find and currently offer into poses that will hide the flaws that a majority of your clients have.

■ FINDING NEW IDEAS

To find new poses to offer to your clients, you need only do two things. First, you must open your mind.

Don't get stuck in a posing rut—look for new posing ideas to make your clients look great.

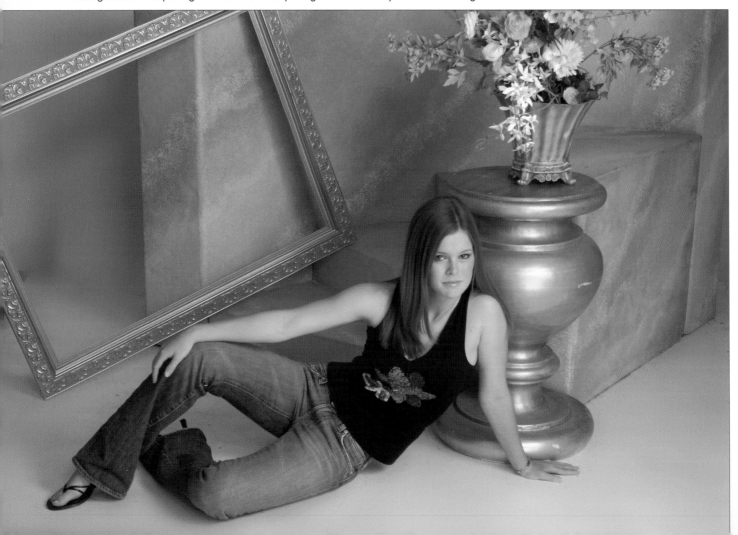

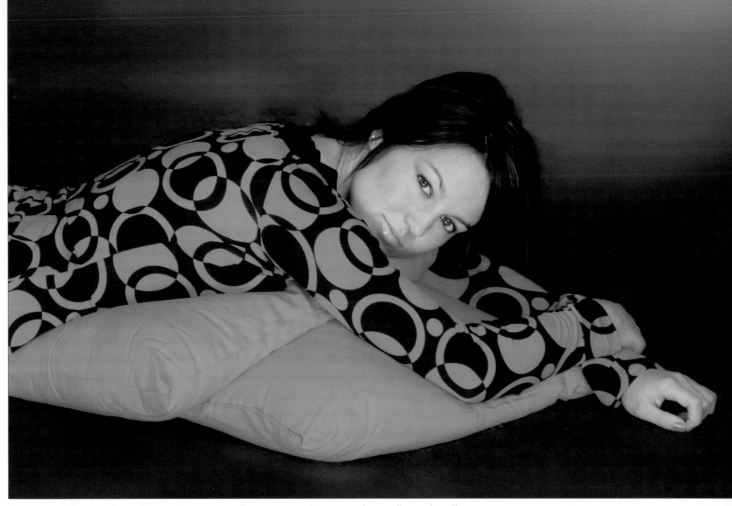
Getting caught up in the "rules" can sometimes close your mind to poses that really work well.

Put out of your mind everything you have learned about posing. The posing manuals that we all learned from are completely outdated by today's standards. When all these rules that we learned were created, the times were different. Women were passive creatures who stayed home and "tended" to their husbands and babies, and men had to look stiff and unemotional. Nowadays, men spend as much time on their hair and getting ready as women do. And if you don't think women have changed, just leave the toilet seat up one time and see what happens—she'll give you "tended to!"

Some photographers are so stuck in what they have always done that they bitterly resist any change. I once took a class on senior portraits. There was another photographer attending this class who was just starting out. Every time the photographer conducting the class wasn't talking, this photographer would ask me all kinds of questions. At lunch, we had some extra time, so, with permission, I went into the camera room and started showing my newfound friend some of the different

poses we use with seniors. He loved it. Everything was going fine until the photographer conducting the program came in. I was doing a yearbook pose that had the subject reclining back, to make the shoulders run diagonally through the frame. The photographer conducting the class remarked that this was a pose more suited to boudoir than seniors. To reply, I simply asked both photographers if the subject looked beautiful in the pose. They both responded affirmatively. I said that was all that mattered.

The moral of the story is that people just want to look great. They want to look natural or glamorous—not like mannequins.

Step one (opening your mind) can be difficult, but step two (finding interesting poses) is easy. Just remember one word—plagiarize! There is no copyright on good ideas. So where do you turn? If you are smart, you start looking at the fashion magazines that are directed toward the market that you work with the most. For our studio, I look at *Seventeen* and *Sassy*, as well as *Cosmo*, *GQ*, and *Mirabella*. Your clients might

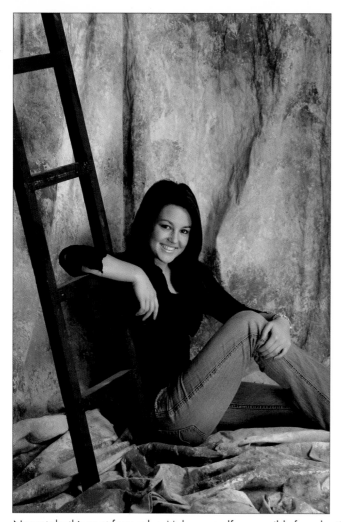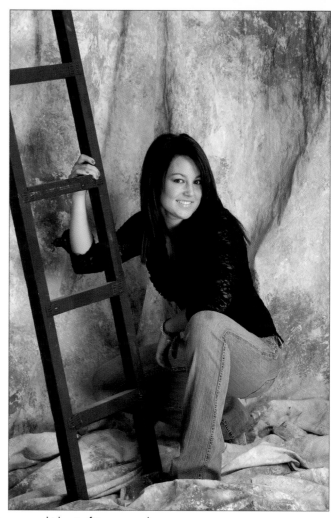

Never take things at face value. Make yourself responsible for adapting a good idea to fit your needs.

have older or (in the case of children) younger tastes and styles, but there is a mountain of creative poses each month in these magazines—and they can be yours for the price of a subscription.

If you work with ladies, from high-school seniors to adults, and have problems with posing women for full-length portraits, get a *Victoria's Secret* catalog. The photographers who work on catalogs like this are masters at making the human form look its best. Naturally, you are not going to be photographing a high school senior in lingerie, but the body can be posed the same way as in the *Victoria's Secret* catalog—the senior girl will just have more clothing on. For those of you who do glamour photography, your client will be in the same poses, only wearing less clothing.

Never take things at face value. Make yourself responsible for adapting a good idea to fit your needs. The most unhappy and unsuccessful people in any pro-

fession, and in life in general, are the ones who consistently look at new ideas and say that they won't work. The happy and truly successful people in the world look at new ideas and think, "It could work—and I think I can make it even better."

We have taken the idea of gathering poses from magazines one step farther. We encourage our seniors to bring in the poses they see in magazines that impress them the most, and we will duplicate the poses for them. This gives us a constant supply of new poses and—even better—they are poses selected by our target market. This tells us exactly what our specific clients want.

For some photographers, getting rid of old poses and ideas is harder than coming up with new ones. All of us love security. We like to know exactly what to do and not have to shoot from the hip or think on our feet. We are always afraid that when we throw something away we may not have what it takes to fill the void that is left. I pride myself on staying current, so nothing stays in our sample books or on the walls of the studio for more than one year. I repaint at least 30 percent of my backgrounds every year and try not to keep any sets more than three years. I make it my goal to paint at least two new backgrounds, design one new set, and have at least two uninterrupted test sessions each month. Seniors are the most style-conscious type of client, but all photographers need to force themselves to bring new ideas into their studios—and to throw out some of the old ones.

■ TEST SESSIONS

An easy way to try out new ideas is by photographing subjects who are not clients. The problem that most photographers have is that they don't plan the test session. They have a person come in to the studio and plan on "winging it." They think to themselves that working off the cuff will raise their creativity. Yeah, right! If you don't plan for your test session, you will almost always end up doing variations on what you already offer—which gets you nowhere. When you schedule a test session with a subject, gather together the clippings clients have given you as well as those you've collected yourself from magazines, books, and other sources. Make yourself a checklist of how many new ideas you want to try and what changes you want to make to each of the ideas you have clippings for. Rarely do ideas spring up

fully formed and ready to use in your situation. You have to make alterations to the ideas so they fit your studio and your client's taste.

■ ADAPTING A POSE TO HIDE A FLAW

We have already looked at the typical flaws that both men and women have. Now, you need to adapt your poses to cover, disguise, or cast a shadow on the areas of the body and face that are problems. Many of the more relaxed poses that you will find already hide some of the most annoying problems that your clients have.

Double Chin. A double chin (or the entire neck area) is easily hidden by resting the chin on the hands, arms, or shoulders. Be careful that the subject barely touches his or her chin down on the supporting element. Resting on it too heavily will alter the jawline.

Another way to make a double chin and loose skin on the neck easier on your client's eyes is to stretch the skin under the neck. To do this, turn the body away from the light, then turn the face back toward the light. This will stretch out the double chin so that it will not be as noticeable.

When a head-and-shoulder pose is needed (for a yearbook, business publication, etc.) it is sometimes impossible to use the hands or arms to hide this problem area. Posing the body to make the neck stretch can only do so much to hide a large double chin. In a case like this, you do what some photographers call the "turkey neck." To do this, have the subject extend their

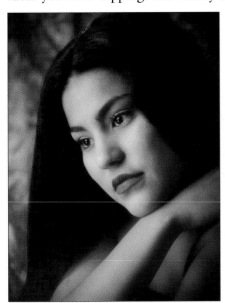 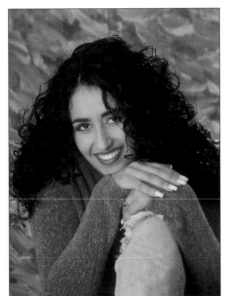 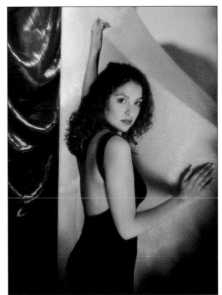

A double chin (or the entire neck area) is easily hidden by resting the chin on the hands, arms, or shoulders.

chin directly toward the camera, which stretches out the double chin. Then have them bring down their face to the proper angle. Most of the time, this eliminates the double chin from view. It is especially helpful when photographing a man who is wearing a shirt and tie.

Men who have large double chins often also have tight collars, which push up the double chin and make it even more noticeable.

Ears. Corrective posing is also the best way to combat the problem of ears that stick out too far.

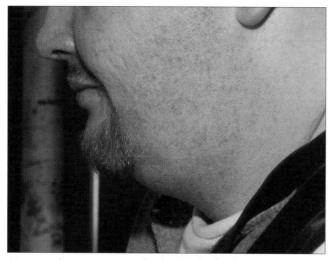 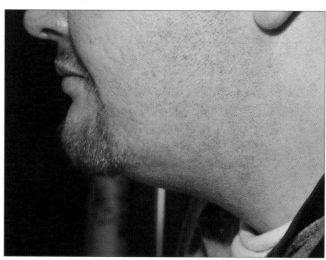

Minimize the appearance of a double chin (left) by having the client stretch his chin forward (right) to stretch out the skin.

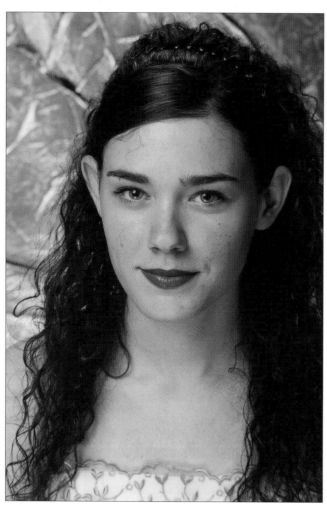 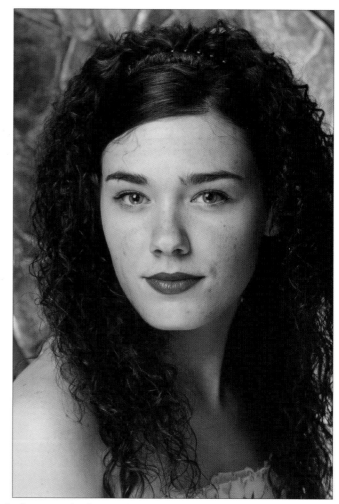

For clients with long hair, bring the hair over the shoulder and around the face to make the ears less visible.

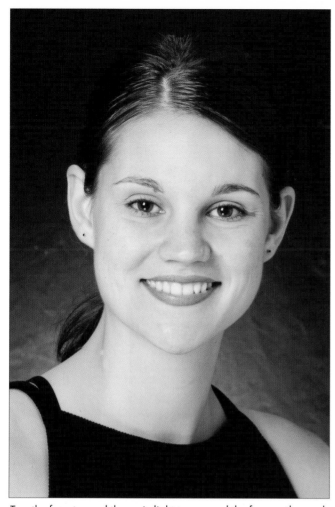 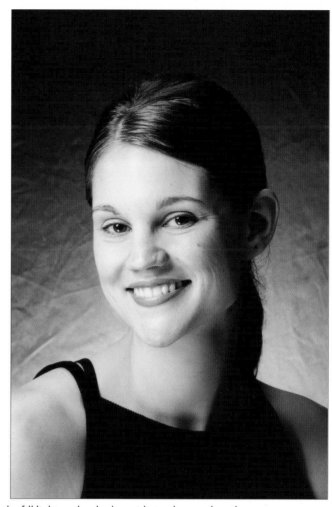

Turn the face toward the main light to conceal the far ear, then reduce the fill light on the shadow side to obscure the other ear.

Ladies who have a problem with their ears usually wear their hair over them. In this case, make sure that the subject's hair isn't tucked behind her ear, as this will make the ears stand out. Larger ears can also stick out through the hair, making them appear really large.

Without hair to conceal them, the best way to reduce the appearance of the ears is to turn the face toward the main light until the ear on the main-light side of the face is obscured from the camera's view. Then, move the fill reflector farther from the subject to increase the shadow on the visible ear, or move the main light more to the side of the subject to create a shadow over the ear. Reducing the separation between the subject and the background in this area will also make the outline of the ear less visible. Overhead hair lights should be turned off to avoid highlighting the top of the ear.

In a situation where the ears are so large that they can't be hidden in this manner, you have two choices:

either let the ears be seen or highlight only the "mask" of the face, letting both sides of the face fall into shadow. This is the type of lighting that Marty Richert made famous years ago.

Noses. The nose is only seen in a portrait because of the shadows that are around it. By turning the face more toward the light or bringing the main light more toward the camera, you can reduce the shadow on the side of the nose and thereby reduce the appearance of the size of the nose.

Butterfly lighting, using the main light directly over the camera and a reflector underneath the subject, can also reduce the apparent size of the nose. This type of lighting compacts the nose by completely eliminating the shadows on each side of it. The only shadow that appears on the face is the butterfly-shaped shadow that appears under the nose, hence the name.

Shininess and the strong highlight that runs down the nose on shiny skin also draws attention to the size

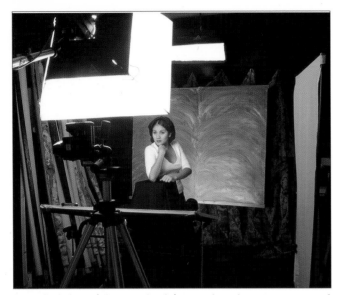

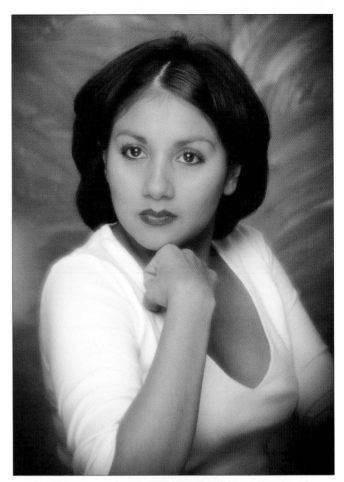

Butterfly lighting (above and right) can reduce the apparent size of the subject's nose. Turning the face toward the main light and directing the eyes back at the camera (bottom right) reveals more of the white of the eye, making the eyes look larger.

of the nose. Usually, this is only a problem with guys (or when working outdoors on very warm days). Ladies usually wear a translucent powder that eliminates this shine. By keeping a few shades of this powder handy you can save yourself a great deal of time in retouching.

Eyes. Eyes are by far the most important part of a person's appearance. Making the eyes appear alive and beautiful is the single most important part of any portrait. The most frequently made mistake of young photographers is lighting and posing a portrait primarily to bring out the structure of the face. Instead, the priority should be to ensure that the subject's eyes have beautiful catchlights in them. This is accomplished through carefully placing the main light each time you change the pose—especially when using the smaller softboxes used in corrective lighting. I have found the easiest way to achieve the perfect illumination with any light is to raise the light to a point that it is obviously too high, then slowly lower it until catchlights appear in the upper eye and the lighting effect is pleasing to the contours of the individual's face.

Remember, no matter how many flaws you correct, if the eyes aren't lit properly, the portrait will look lifeless. Here are some additional tips:

1. Never have a subject look at an inanimate object (like the camera lens). Instead, have them look

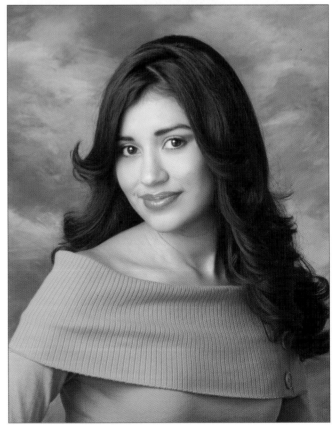

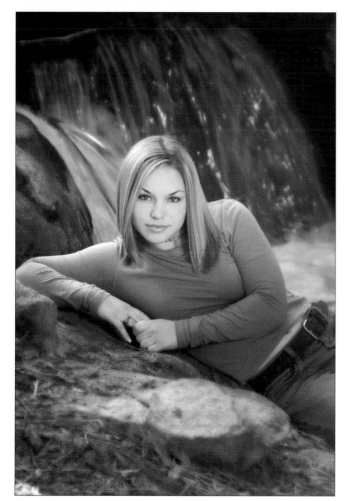

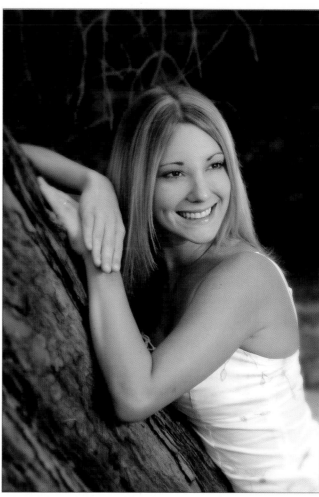

Turn the eyes toward the camera for a more direct look (left). Turn the eyes away from the camera for a more reflective look (right).

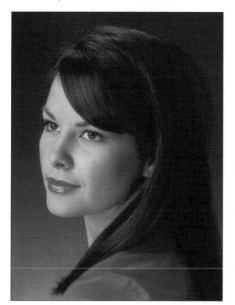

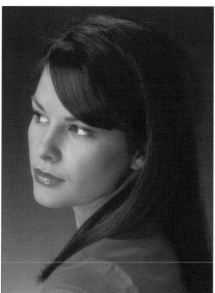

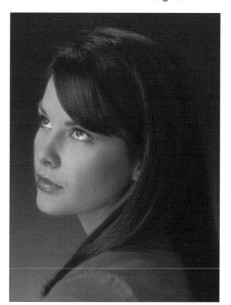

For reflective portraits, the eyes should follow the line of the nose (left). Avoid allowing the subject's nose to go past the line of the cheek that is farthest from the camera. When the eyes don't follow the nose, the subject looks as though she was distracted just before you clicked the shutter (center and right).

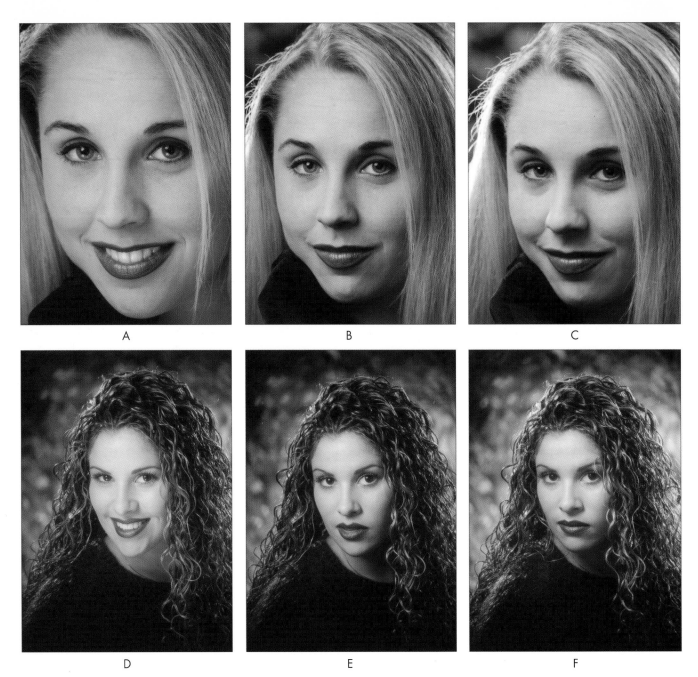

A	B	C
D	E	F

Which would you choose? In C and F, the main light is too high to properly illuminate the eye. This is what happens when you don't adjust the light for each individual pose and client. In B and E, the eyes are lit properly, but the lighting lacks the style and glamour of A and D, where reflected light was added from the mylar top of a drafting table.

at a person. This makes the eyes more alive, because there is someone there to connect with.

2. Make sure that your subject's eyes follow the line of their nose. If they don't, the subject will looks as though someone called their name right before the portrait was taken and they didn't want to move their head.

3. Never let the subject's nose go past the line of the cheek that is the farthest from the camera.

Corrective posing can also help a client who has eyes that are either too small or too large. Most people want their eyes to look as large as possible. By turning the face to the side (toward the main light) and bringing the subject's gaze back to the camera, the pupil of the eye goes more toward the corner of the eye opening and gives the eye more impact as well as a larger appearance. Be sure to position the main light to create nice catchlights. With a person with larger eyes that tend to bulge, the face needs to be directed more toward the camera. You must also make sure that no catchlight appears on the whites of the eye, as this will draw a great deal of attention to this area and make it much too bright.

Glasses. Glasses will always be a problem if you don't advise your clients to get empty frames from their eye doctors. Nonreflective lenses make life a little easier, but anytime there is glass in a pair of frames, you end up lighting and posing the subject to make the glasses look good, rather than to make the subject look good.

In our studio, we use a light or reflector under the subject to add a more glamorous look to the lighting, as well as to bring out more of the eye color and smooth the complexion. With any type of glass in the glasses, the light or reflector has to be removed or it will create glare.

Another technique used to reduce glass glare is to angle the frames of the glasses so that the lenses point slightly downward and the frame raises slightly above the ear. This usually reduces the glare and the change of angle isn't noticeable from the perspective of the camera. This isn't an ideal solution, but it is more manageable than spending a fortune on enhancement to remove the glare.

A second effective technique is simply to raise the main light to a point at which no glare is visible from the angle of the camera. Here again, though, you are creating the portrait to avoid glass glare, not to make your client look her best.

Expressions. Proper expression depends on the age of your clients. With babies and small children, parents love laughing smiles. With children, moody, more serious expressions are salable. In dealing with teens and adults, the best expressions are more subtle.

While squinty eyes are cute on a baby, not many adults really want to see themselves with no eyes, huge chubby cheeks, and every tooth in their mouth visible. Large smiles are not only unflattering to adults for these reasons but also because this expression brings out every line and wrinkle on a person's face. Adults are always self-conscious about crow's feet, smile lines, and bags under the eyes—all of which are made much more noticeable by huge smiles. While retouching can lessen these lines on the face, the retouching often reduces the lines too much, resulting in subjects that don't look like themselves.

Expression isn't your client's responsibility. As the photographer, you must develop a connection with your subjects that allows them to feel comfortable enough with you that they will "mirror" your expression. When you want a relaxed expression, speak to your clients in a relaxed tone of voice, with a relaxed, nonsmiling expression. When you want your clients to smile, simply speak to them in more upbeat tones and smile yourself. The client will follow your lead.

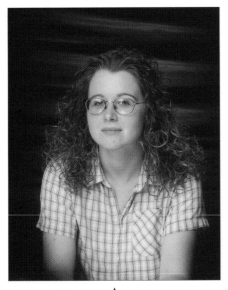

A

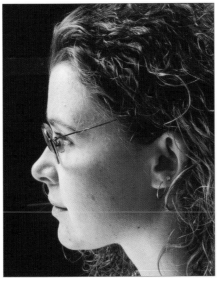

B

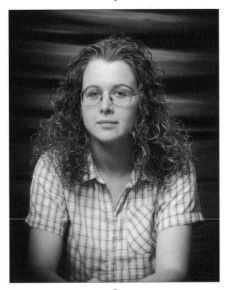

C

Glare from glasses is always a problem (A). One solution is to angle the frames so the glass points slightly down (B). From the perspective of the camera, this tilt isn't noticeable and eliminates the glare (C).

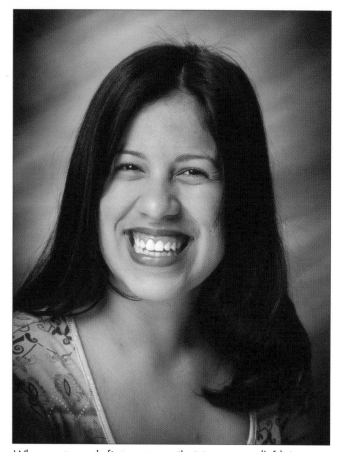 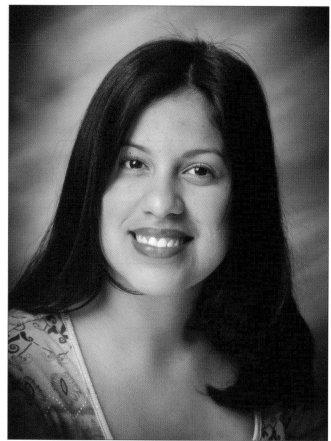

When most people first start to smile, it is enormous (left). A moment after a person smiles that laughing smile, the expression starts to relax (right). This is the expression adults prefer.

With smiling, timing is important. It is easy to get a subject to smile, but once your client smiles, it is up to you to decide when the perfect smile occurs and take the pictures. When most people first start to smile, it is enormous. If you take the shot at this point, you end up with a laughing or almost-laughing smile. Once your client has a smile like this, you must watch and wait. A moment after a person smiles that laughing smile, the expression starts to relax. It isn't that big a change, but it is the difference between a laughing smile and a smile that is pleasing to an adult client.

Baldness. If a client is bald by choice, meaning they have decided to shave their head, they will not usually be that self-conscious about it. To photograph them, simply turn off your hair light and you will be fine.

However, if a person's baldness is out of his control, no matter what he says, he is not altogether too happy about it. When you meet with a man over thirty who is wearing a hat or cap you can be 90-percent certain there is a bald head underneath. To use shadow to reduce the appearance of the balding area, turn off the hair light and lower the camera angle slightly. Then, make sure that the separation light is low enough to just define the shoulders from the background but still allow the top of the head to blend in. At this point, the problem will be much less noticeable.

If a man is really worried about his lack of hair, you can lower the main light and use a gobo in front of the main light source to hold back some of the light coming from the top of the light modifier. They (and you) have to remember, this isn't an alternative for a hair transplant, though. It doesn't make a person appear to have hair, it just makes the problem less noticeable.

Arms. Most women worry about their upper arms appearing too large or about hair showing on their forearms. Men generally worry about their arms looking too thin or too flabby. The best way to avoid problems with arms is to cover them up with long sleeves. When short sleeves are worn, your choices are: compose the portrait above the problem area; use lighting falloff or vignettes to make the area darker and less

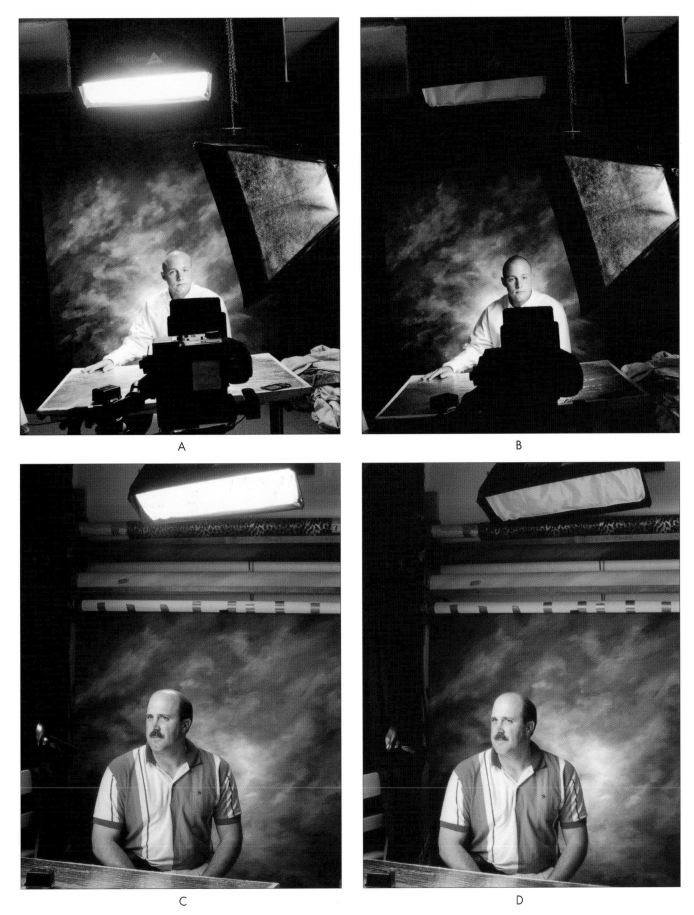

When photographing a subject who is bald by choice (A and B) turn off the hair light to prevent the top of his head from glowing. Combine this lighting trick with a lowered camera angle to help disguise the problem for clients who are not bald by choice (C and D).

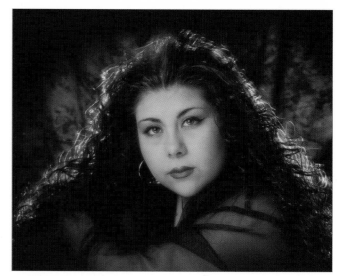
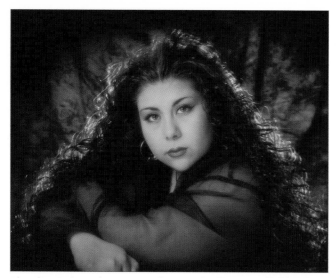

The client's sheer sleeves reveal too much of her arms (left). Achieving a more flattering look (right) was as simple as composing the image with a closer view. Notice how the subject's long hair was also pulled across her shoulder to help disguise the problem area.

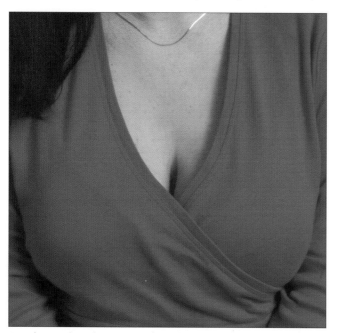
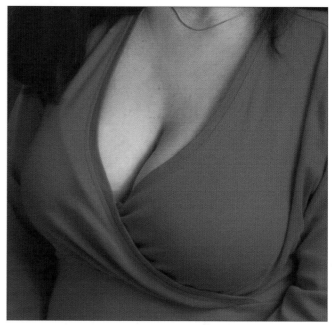

Simply turn the subject away from the main light to increase the shadows that enhance the shape of the bust.

noticeable; or, if the client has long hair, use the hair to soften the problem area.

Bustline. The bustline isn't a problem in most portraits, but you must make sure that it appears even if it will be noticeable in the frame.

When a low-cut top is worn, the size of the bustline is determined by the appearance of cleavage. Cleavage is nothing but a shadow. Increase the shadow by turning the subject toward the shadow side of the frame and you will, in turn, increase the apparent size of the bustline. There are times when a top is too low-cut for the type of portraits a client wants. By turning the client toward the main light, the shadow in the cleavage area is reduced.

Waistline. The waistline is the area that almost everyone feels is never thin enough. To make the waistline appear more slim, turn the client toward the shadow side of the frame. This works well as long as the person has a somewhat flat stomach. If you do this with a person who has a bulging stomach, you will put the bulge in silhouette. This is like doing a profile of a person with a big nose.

When someone does have a tummy bulge, the easiest way to hide the stomach area is to pose the client in a sitting position, then elevate the leg closest to the camera. This partially obscures the stomach area. Having subjects rest an elbow on their knee (or knees) will completely hide this area.

However, sitting positions cause significant waist problems of their own—even for thin people. When the subject is in a seated position, their clothing and skin wrinkle over the waistband of their pants, giving even the thinnest person a roll at the waistline—whether it be of cloth or skin. If the person is thin, have her straighten her back, almost to the point of arching it, to correct the problem—as shown in the images below. If the person is heavier, hide this area as described above.

Thighs and Legs. Thighs and legs need to appear as thin and toned as possible. This isn't a problem for most men, because it's normally only athletic men who ask to take a photograph in clothing that shows their legs or thighs. Women, however, are often told they should wear dresses, tight skirts, and tight pants—even when it would be in their best interest not to.

When posing female subjects in a full-length pose, I always have the person sitting or laying down. Unless

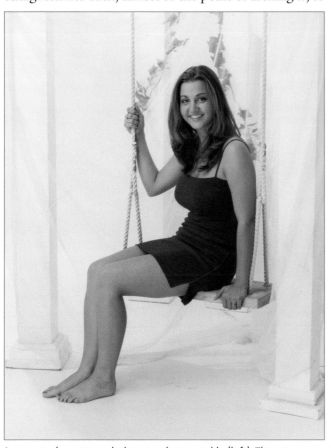 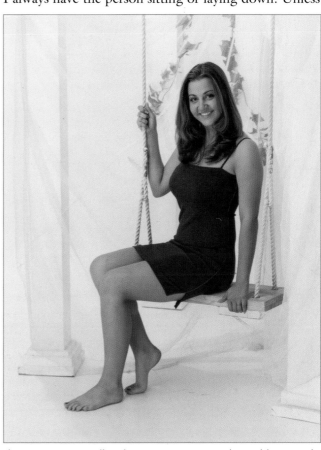

In a seated position, clothing tends to wrinkle (left). This gives even the thinnest person a roll at their waist. To correct the problem, simply have her straighten her back, almost to the point of arching it (right).

TARGETING TEST SESSIONS AND DISPLAYS

If a majority of the money in your pocket is made from weddings, the majority of portraits on display in your business should be weddings and a majority of the test sessions you do should be scheduled with a bride and groom. The same is true for families, children, and seniors. I have visited so many studios that make most of their living from weddings yet show black & white portraits of aspiring models all over their studio. I know of some photographers who work with mature clients in a variety of situations (families, business portraits, weddings, etc.) and when they do a test session it is always of a young woman in swimwear or lingerie. This is, first of all, a little creepy—and probably why so many photographers get a less-than-sterling reputation. More importantly, it does you and your business no good. You can't learn to work more effectively with one type of client by photographing different type of test subject.

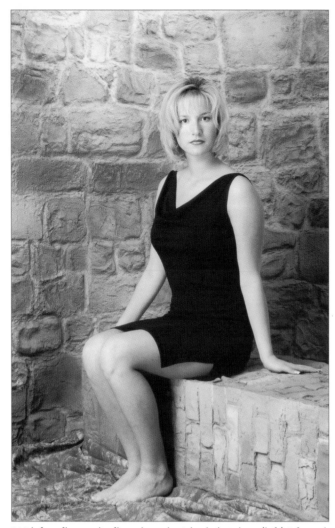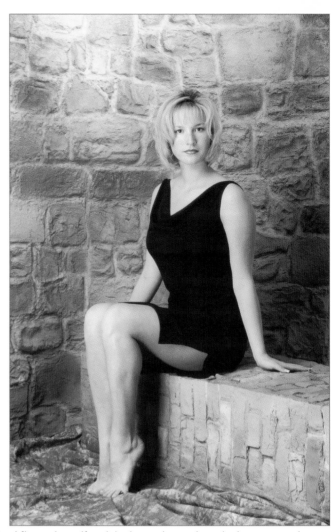

With feet flat on the floor, legs don't look their best (left). Lifting the heel flexes the calf and thigh muscles, making the legs appear longer and firmer. This can be accomplished by wearing high heels, or simply lifting the heel into the same position as if the subject were wearing high heels (right).

a person is very tall and thin, she will always look better posed in this way. Whenever I have a woman seated, no matter how thin or heavy she is, I don't have her sit flat on her bottom. Instead, I have her roll onto the hip that is closest to the camera. This is slimming, because it hides a good portion of the seat and thigh areas behind the subject.

Anytime the legs are going to be showing and not covered with pants, have the subject wear the tallest heels she owns. There is a reason why women who want to have the greatest impact when wearing a dress wear very high heels. When the heel is pushed up, it flexes the calf and thigh muscle, making the legs appear longer and firmer.

If the woman is going barefoot, have her push up her heels just as high-heeled shoes would do.

CHAPTER FIVE

CLOTHING SELECTION

Most photographers have gotten to a point where they coordinate the basic color of a client's clothing to that of the background, set, or outdoor scene. Darker tones of clothing are paired with darker backgrounds. Lighter tones of clothing are paired with a lighter background. This makes the viewer's eye focus on the person and not what the person is wearing. It also gives you the ability to hide body size, because you don't create an exact outline of the client's body as you would with a white dress on a black background. To create a portrait that has a sense of style, however, you not only need to coordinate the color of the clothing to the scene, but also the style of the cloth-

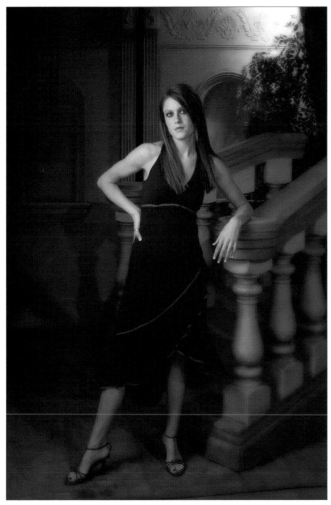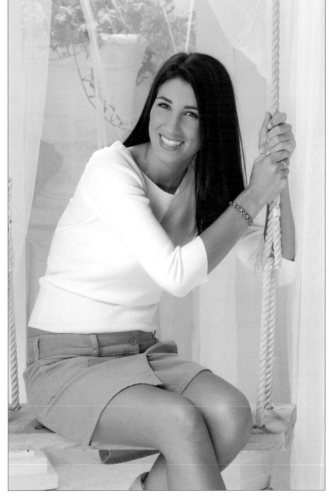

Pairing dark clothes with darker settings and light clothes with lighter settings helps keep the emphasis on the person. It also makes it easier to disguise common figure problems by letting the body blend in with the background.

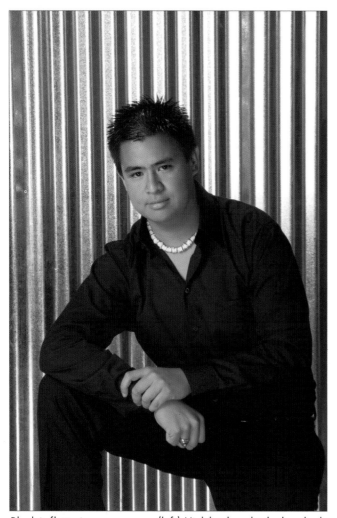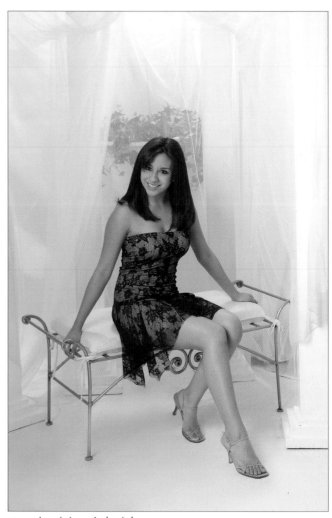

Black is flattering on everyone (left). High heels make the legs look more toned and shapely (right).

ing, which must present a similar feeling to that reflected in the scene. Although correcting flaws is important to the client, the portrait must also visually "make sense." This can only happen when each aspect of the portrait complements the other.

■ CLOTHING GUIDELINES

Probably the best advice I can give you in regard to your clients' clothing is to have them bring in everything for you to look at. I am not kidding. We tell our seniors to bring in everything, and they do. The average girl brings in ten to twenty-five outfits; the average guy brings five to ten. By doing this, you always have other choices when a favorite outfit is a bad choice for a particular subject.

Long Sleeves. We stress the importance of bringing in the proper styles of clothing. We suggest long sleeves for all portraits that are to be taken from the waist up. Large arms are much less noticeable in a full-length pose, so short sleeves are less of a problem in these portraits.

Black Clothing. We also suggest that anyone who worries about weight should bring in a variety of darker colors of clothing and several choices that are black. Black clothing is amazing. It will take ten to thirty pounds off of anyone who wears it, provided you use common sense and pair it with a black or very dark background. If you are photographing a family and Dad has a "beer belly," ask him to wear a black sweater. Unless his stomach is huge, it will appear flat in the final portrait. If Mom has larger hips, put her in a black skirt or dress and she will appear noticeably thinner.

High Heels. Anytime a woman will be in a dress, we ask her to bring in the highest heel she owns to wear with it. If she doesn't have any 3-inch heels, she can borrow them from a friend. If the legs are showing, panty hose should be worn unless the subject has very tan legs with great muscle tone. The nylons will not only make the legs look better by darkening them, but will make them appear firmer and disguise signs of cellulite.

■ COMMON PROBLEMS

With clothing, the easiest way to know *what* to do is to know what *not to* do. If you think in terms of all the problems that clothing can create for your clients and then help them avoid these problems, you will learn how to use your clients' clothing to make them look their best. Here are some common problems that should be avoided.

Too-Tight or Too-Loose Clothing. We warn clients against wearing jeans or pants that are too tight around the waist. These create a roll where the tight waistband cuts into the stomach. Tight clothing also affects the subject's ability to pose comfortably. I have had some subjects turn beet red because of tight pants as they try to get into a pose. For this reason, we ask all of our clients to bring in a comfortable pair of shorts (or, in the winter, sweatpants), to make it as easy as possible to get into the poses that won't show areas below the waist.

If women have a frequent problem with tight jeans, guys (especially young guys) have the baggies. This cool-looking (so they think) style has the crotch that hangs down to their knees, while at the same time revealing undergarments to the world. Just try to pose a client in a seated position when there are three yards of material stretched out between his legs! Try to have him put his hands in pants pockets that are hanging so low he can't even reach them.

In general, clothing that is loose-fitting on a person who is thin or athletic will add weight to the person in the portrait, especially if it is loose at the waist or hips. Tight clothing will add weight to those people who are heavier. With tight clothing on a heavy person you can see tummy bulges, cellulite, lines from waistbands, and every other flaw that weight brings to the human body.

Wrong Undergarments. Many women forget to bring in the proper undergarments. They bring light-colored clothing, but only have a black bra and underwear. They bring in a top with no straps or spaghetti straps and they don't have a strapless bra. In this case, they either have to have the straps showing or not wear a bra, which for most women isn't a good idea.

Guys are no better. I can't count the number of times I have had a guy show up with a dark suit and nothing but white socks. Some men (okay, *most* men) tend to be more sloppy than women, which means that the clothing they bring often looks like it has been stored in a big ball at the bottom of their closet for the last three months. Many show up with clothing that used to fit ten years ago when it was actually in fashion.

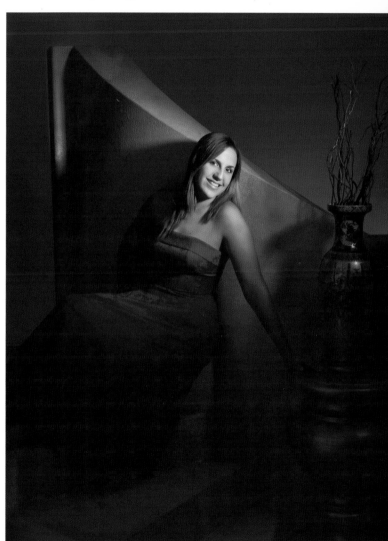

Advise your subjects to bring the correct undergarments for each outfit. For example, strapless dresses require strapless bras.

CHAPTER SIX

CORRECTING FLAWS WITH THE SCENE

The scene or setting can often be one of the most effective tools you have for correcting clients' flaws. As you have seen, letting the body blend into the background can make problem areas like large hips or a balding head much less noticeable. This works well in low-key portraits, but when you start working with high-key settings (or even with the client in light-colored clothing), the problem area is still obvious. But, just as with poses that use the knee, arm, or leg to disguise a problem, elements in the scene can also be used to conceal flaws.

■ USING THE FOREGROUND

Most scenes give you ways to hide flaws by using the foreground. Although it is often overlooked, making

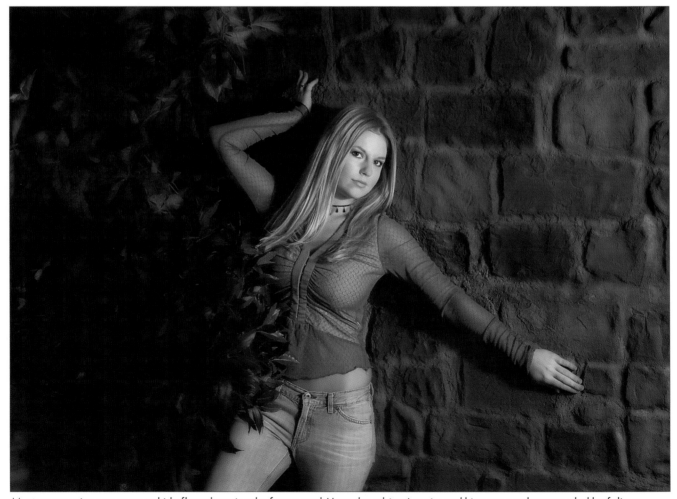

Most scenes give you ways to hide flaws by using the foreground. Here, the subject's waist and hips are partly concealed by foliage.

use of the foreground not only gives you the ability to hide a client's flaws but, from an artistic standpoint, provides a greater ability to create the illusion of depth in your portraits. By using an element in the foreground, the subject in critical focus, and then a background that recedes farther and farther from the subject, you have a built-in sense of depth.

When it comes to correcting a client's flaws, it is amazing how even a simple foreground element like a plant or a few columns can soften or hide a large hip, tummy bulge, large upper arm, or hairy forearm. Whether you have something as simple as a client sitting backwards in a chair, or an entire set arranged to hide problem areas, it is a very effective way to give clients a version of reality they can live with.

Learning how to coordinate foreground elements with the background can be challenging. Whether you are using a painted background, seamless paper, or a projection screen, ultimately it's a two-dimensional surface—even if it's styled to create the illusion of depth. You can enhance the feeling of depth by using multiple elements in the foreground placed at different distances between the camera and subject. You can also add more elements in between the subject and the background.

The hardest part of using foreground elements is coordinating the style, look, and color with the other parts of the scene. A plant or tree is often used in the foreground because it is easy. It goes with just about everything and it doesn't take any time to prepare. Chairs are also a popular choice for the foreground element. Either one can be effective.

We have found many background and foreground elements at the local home store. For example, I purchased a French door on clearance for $10. We have also purchased ladders, steel grates, tin roofing material, and many other interesting foreground and background items at this type of store. You are only limited by your imagination and your time to shop around. When I first opened my studio, like most new photographers, I had all kinds of time but very little money to purchase sets. Now, with over 3000 seniors to photograph each year, my writing, and my family, I have much more money than I do time to look for background items, so I tend to purchase them from set manufacturers.

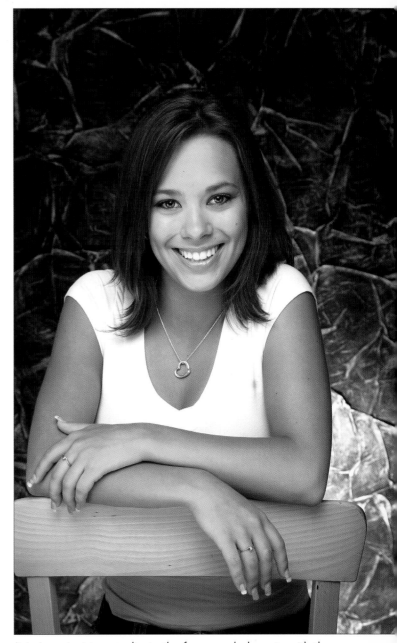

It is important to coordinate the foreground elements with the background and clothing to create a unified look.

As you start working with sets, whether you purchase them or create your own, you need to look for unique ways to use the components. The average photographer sees an arch at a trade show. He buys it, brings it into his studio, and it remains a single arch for all time. Yet, in addition to being an arch, it is also three individual pieces that can be combined with other set components to create multiple looks. This gives you the most for your money—and it also provides opportunities to improve your photographs and hide your clients' flaws.

CHAPTER SEVEN

OUTDOOR PORTRAITS

As photographers have long known, a session shot on location (or partially on location) will have a higher sales average than a session done in the studio alone. Yet, many photographers avoid the great outdoors like the plague—and for good reason.

■ LIGHTING

While outdoor sessions can boost profits, working outside gives you little control over your lighting—at least the kind of control needed for corrective lighting. We are all taught that to achieve the best possible portraits outdoors we have to get up at the crack of dawn or stay out until it is almost dark. We have all been told that the ideal lighting exists for an hour-and-a-half window after sunrise and your next opportunity starts an hour and a half before sunset. Realistically, this give you just two short windows of opportunity per day.

To boost our profits by scheduling outdoor shoots, we needed to learn how to work with the natural light as it changed throughout the day. This took some getting used to. Like most photographers, I had used flash for outdoor group portraits at weddings, but the flash all but destroyed the feeling of the soft, warm, outdoor light that exists naturally. Therefore, flash was not an option I preferred.

The better option was to manipulate the existing light with a combination of reflectors and black panels, what Leon Kennamar used to call "subtractive lighting." Now, as we venture into the great outdoors, we use the light that exists and modify it to fit the situation. Since we specialize in seniors, the techniques we use are designed for photographing a single person, but the principles will work on a couple or a small group.

Working with midday light, you will find two different lighting situations. The first scene (the ideal one) occurs when you get lucky and find in one location an obstruction that blocks the light from directly overhead (under a tree with branches overhead, or on a porch with the roof overhead, for example), and a second obstruction on one side or the other at ground level. This creates a shadow area and a large, directional light source to act as the main light.

In the second type of scene, one or more of the key elements needed to create the ideal scene is missing. In

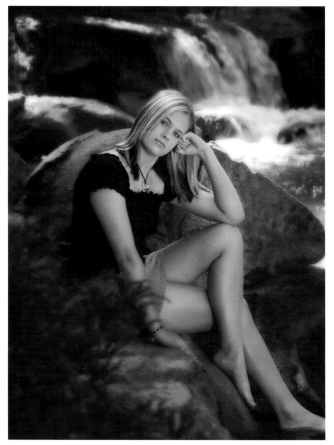

Outdoor scenes offer many good foreground elements.

this case, you must identify what is needed to create portrait-quality lighting and use black panels and reflectors to fix the problems. For more on outdoor portrait photography, refer to one of the best books ever written on the subject (if, as the author, I do say so myself), called *Outdoor and Location Portrait Photography*, from Amherst Media.

■ USE OF SHADOW

When it comes to corrective lighting for outdoor portraits, the use of shadow can soften flaws. Shadow is also the element missing from most photographers' outdoor portraits. Most outdoor portraits I see have a main light source that is too large and wraps light around the entire face. This type of light makes the face look wide and without structure. By placing a black panel on one side of the subject, a shadow is created and the face appears thinner. This also creates a shadow side of the portrait to turn the body toward in order to hide flaws.

■ EYES AND DIRECTION OF LIGHT

The eyes are the best indicator of light direction and the modifications that need to be made. What you are looking for is one large, well-defined catchlight in the upper half of each eye. This catchlight should be to one side or the other of the pupil and positioned in the colored portion of the eye.

If the catchlights are too large, extending from one side of the pupil to the other, or if you see two distinct catchlights, you'll need to modify the source of light or change your subject's position. First, try turning your subject away from the source of natural light (probably the open sky) until the catchlights are in the proper position. If turning the subject doesn't eliminate the second catchlight or reduce the size of the catchlight enough, you can bring in a black panel. Simply place the black panel in front and to the side of the subject to eliminate the second catchlight or reduce the size of the natural main-light source.

■ USING MIRRORS AND TRANSLUCENT PANELS

If you don't have the perfect light, create it. Outdoors, to produce light that is as close as possible to that from

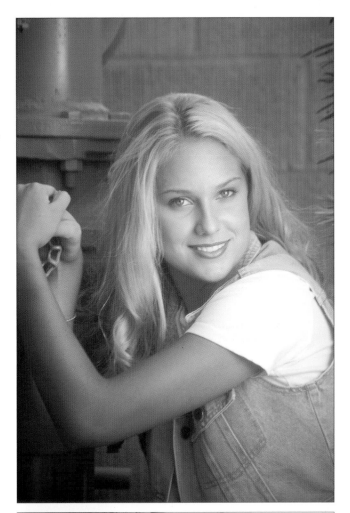

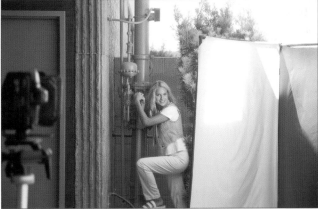

To create soft, natural light outdoors, use a mirror to reflect light through a translucent panel placed in the main-light position.

softboxes in the studio, use mirrors and translucent panels. In this setup, a large mirror functions as the main light and is positioned to reflect direct sunlight through a translucent panel placed in between it and the subject. I also like to have some light coming from underneath the subject for a more glamorous look, so we place a second smaller mirror to pass direct sunlight

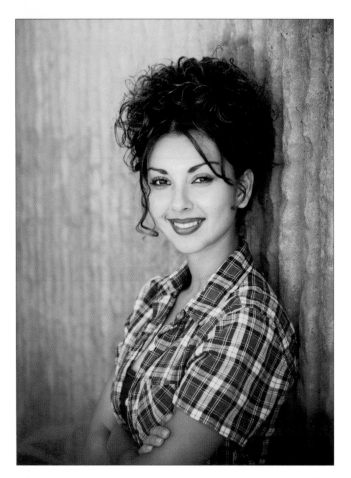

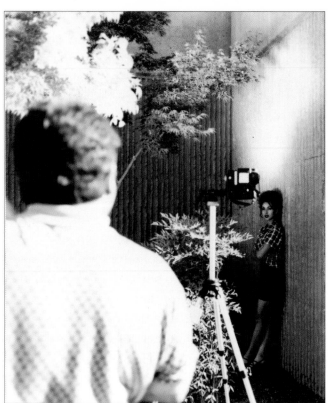

Feathering raw light can make it usable for the main light of a portrait. As you can see, the beam of reflected light is on the wall just above the subject's head.

through a translucent panel in a lower position. It's softer than a reflector and completely controllable.

■ POSITIONING A REFLECTOR

There are two times when you will need to use a reflector. The first is to add, but not overpower, the natural main light. The second use is to produce catchlights in the eyes, turning the reflector into the main light. However, simply reflecting direct sunlight onto a subject's face with a silver or gold reflector provides a less-than-photographic quality light—not to mention that it's inhumane. To make this intense, raw light usable for the main light of a portrait, you must feather it, just like you would in the studio. To feather the light from a reflector, angle the direct beam of light so it is near but not on the subject. As you get this direct beam of light closer to the subject, you will see the amount of light on the subject increase.

■ USING THE OUTDOOR SCENE EFFECTIVELY

Working at an outdoor location gives you great opportunities to hide your clients' flaws. Although you have less precise control over the lighting, you have many elements to use in the foreground and background to soften the outline of the subject's body.

Hiding White Socks and Bare Feet. A client comes out and despite everything you have told him, he has a white pair of socks gleaming out of a dark pant leg. The solutions are many. You can look for tall grass to pose him in, so you won't see the white socks. You can angle the shot so that a tree branch or other foliage in the foreground covers the area of the white socks. The same ideas can be used to hide a girl's feet if she wants to go barefoot but either hasn't painted her nails or has painted them a bright color.

Arms. The identical technique can be used when you have a young lady with large arms who hasn't listened to your instructions and has brought along nothing but sleeveless tops. Look for foliage in the foreground that is at the proper height and comes into the frame at the proper angle to cover a portion of her arms.

Many times a scene is perfect, but there is no foliage or other element in the foreground to soften or hide a problem area. At this point, you'll need to go to a tree and do a little "constructive pruning." Snatch a branch off of a nearby tree and add it into the frame of the portrait where you need it to hide the flaw.

■ SELECTING A SCENE

To work effectively outdoors, many photographers need to relearn how to locate an appropriate scene. To find the perfect scene, you must first determine the most important quality of a scene for taking portraits. Is it a location with perfect light? Most photographers would think so, but they would be wrong. I can create beautiful light, so to select a scene based only on the quality of light would be a mistake.

What about the quality of shadow? Is there an obstruction above the subject to block the light from overhead, avoiding "raccoon eyes," and an obstruction to one side of the subject to create a shadow area in the portrait? This can thin the face and body, but I can create shadow wherever I want it so, again, to make this the determining factor in scene selection would be a mistake.

What about the appearance of the scene? When you are working in the middle of the day, usable backgrounds or scenes are in short supply, but no matter how perfect the scene is, no matter how perfect the light or shadow, if you have a girl who is overweight and you don't do anything to make her look thinner, all of your work is for nothing, because in all likelihood she will not order.

In this image, notice how the clothing, pose, setting, and lighting work together. When a portrait is well planned, everything in the frame draws your eye toward the subject's face.

The first priority when you are looking for a spot to use corrective techniques is to determine what element are available for hiding your clients' flaws. Once this is determined, you can work at sorting everything else out. If the background is in sunlight, you'll need to add light from a reflector, or mirrored light can be passed through a translucent panel to balance the lighting on the subject with that of the background. If you don't have enough shadow, bring in black panels to create shade.

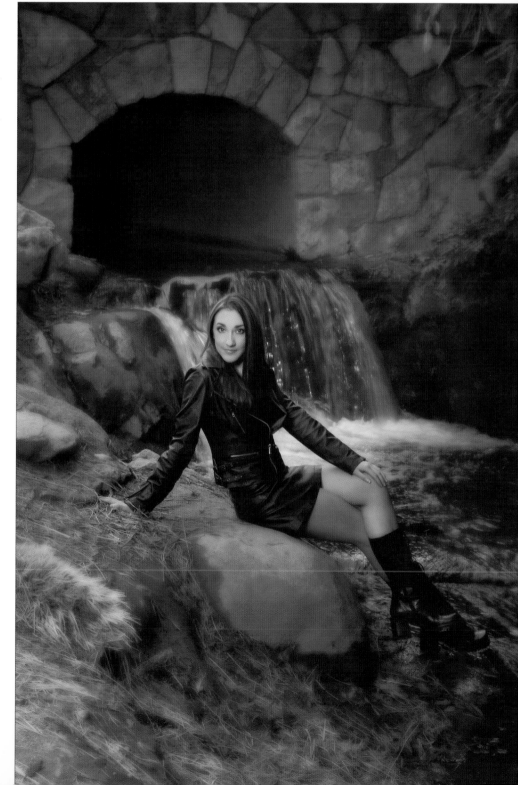

CHAPTER EIGHT

DIGITAL RETOUCHING: WHO PAYS THE BILL?

Now that you've done everything in your power to pose and light your subject in a way that corrects any areas of concern in their appearance, you can go on to consider how digital imaging can further improve your images. This is still a relatively new step in most photographers' workflow—and it represents a significant new expense. So who will pay for the time it takes to retouch or enhance your images? The answer to that question could easily determine whether or not you are in business five years from now. Do you correct *everything* for the price you charge for an 8x10-inch print? Do you provide only simple retouching for acne, wrinkles, and circles under the eyes for the print price, then offer more extensive retouching that is billed directly to the client? Do you bill *all* retouching to the client?

■ PRICING

The answers to the above questions should be determined, in part, based on how you price your work. If you charge $100 to $200 for an 8x10-inch print, you will probably include all the needed retouching and enhancement in the price of the print. At those prices, you would probably have few clients who would be willing pay for additional enhancement. If you price your work in the $40 to $100 range for an 8x10-inch print, you would probably want to include basic clean-up for acne, lines, and circles, then bill out any major enhancement costs to the client. If you price your 8x10-inch prints from $15 to $40, hopefully you don't include much retouching at all—at that price, there's not enough profit to cover the time needed to do retouching (unless, of course, you sell thirty 8x10-inch prints of the same image).

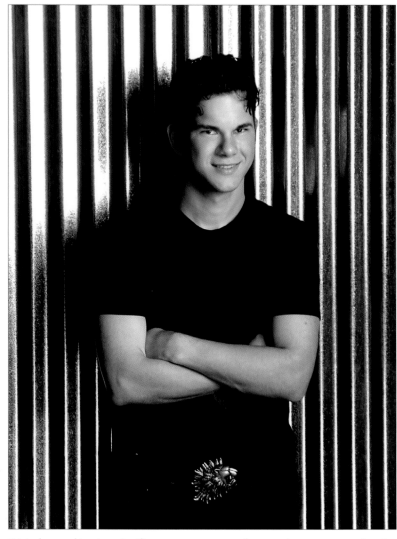

Digital retouching is a significant expense—so who pays it, you or your client?

Valuable time is spent on making digital enhancements, so you don't want to just cover the cost, you have to make a profit on the service.

Most studios that offer lower-end pricing have a "pose charge" or "retouching fee" to cover the cost of basic retouching. More extensive retouching is then billed by the hour in fifteen-minute increments. For a fair billing rate, simply call your lab and ask what they charge for digital enhancement. When setting our prices, we determined that our lab charged $60 an hour for digital correction, so we adopted this rate for our work at the studio. Whether a job takes three minutes or thirteen minutes, the client pays for fifteen minutes. This averages out so that the jobs on which you quote too little time are covered by those that don't require the entire fifteen-minute allotment. Remember, valuable time is spent on enhancement, so you don't want to just cover the cost, you have to make a profit on the service—just like your lab would.

■ WHAT'S INCLUDED
Of course, the problem that most photographers have isn't setting up a way to *offer* their retouching services, it is explaining to the client what is *included* in the service. If you sell your 8x10-inch prints for $100 and vaguely tell the client that the images are complete enhanced, what do you do when the client looks at the final image and tells you they appear too fat in the photograph and you need to fix it? How many rolls and chins can you stretch and cover for $100 and still make a decent profit?

I have people come into the studio every day who think we can fix anything with the click of a mouse. They don't understand that although almost any cor-

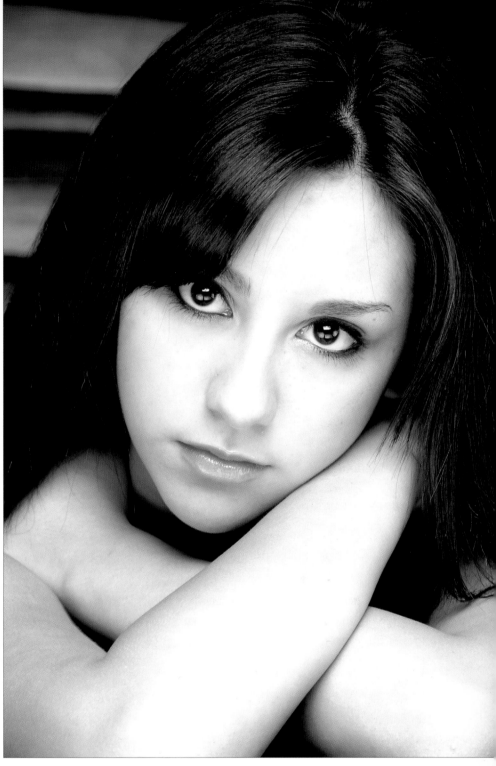

rection *can* be done, many corrections simply take too long to be cost effective. Communication is the key here. You have to inform your client, in writing, about what you *do* include and what you *don't* include in your print price. If you charge a retouching fee, you have to outline very carefully what retouching this covers and give examples of work that isn't included.

In our studios, we work with high-school seniors. Seniors have traditionally been offered a lower price per

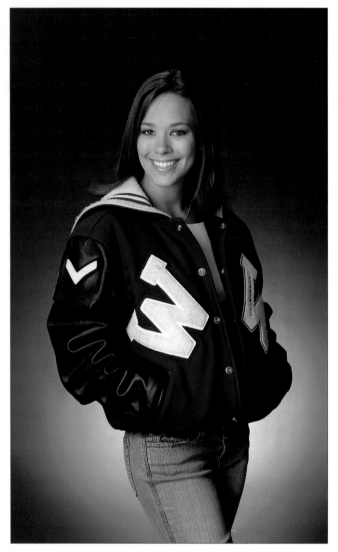

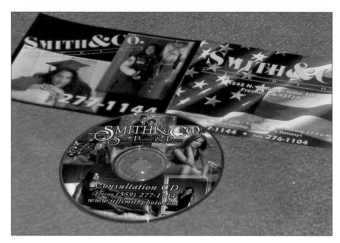

When seniors call to make their appointment, they are sent a brochure and consultation CD, which explains what to bring in and how to plan for their session.

8x10-inch print due to the fact that they purchase a package. I am not the person who came up with the idea, I just have to live with it and find a way to make the best profit I can. Because of this, we include a "pose-change charge" or "image fee." This covers basic cleanup of the face—eliminating acne, softening lines and wrinkles, and removing the darkness under the eyes. The fee is the same whether the person has one zit, no zits, or a face as red as a beet from acne scars—and the client does not have the option to eliminate the fee if they don't want retouching.

Anytime you impose a pose-change charge, as is common in most senior-portrait studios, you will have frugal parents who don't want to pay it. You will get comments like, "She looks good enough!" or "They don't need retouching on that pose!" or "These are just for her friends!" To avoid this confrontation, we call this charge an image fee and explain that it covers the color correction, testing, *and* retouching of each image. This is a legitimate statement, because often the color correction and testing do take longer than the actual retouching—and with senior packages, unlike normal portraiture, the first print isn't priced significantly higher in order to cover these costs.

■ COMMUNICATION

In my experience, most problems that arise between a business owner and a client are nothing more than a lack of communication. I believe in over-communication with my clients. When they call to make their appointment, they are sent a brochure and consultation CD, which explains what to bring in and how to plan for their session. It also discusses what retouching is, what is retouched, and what isn't. It gives examples of

---

NEVER SKIP RETOUCHING

The one thing that is even more damaging to your business than not charging enough for retouching is letting any image go out of your studio without retouching. Every image that leaves your studio is a representation of your work and forms your reputation in the community. If you let work go out that has blemishes and doesn't represent the best that you can do for your client, you are shooting yourself in the foot.

bad choices, like wearing glasses that have glass in them, and informs them as to how much the retouching for this type of mistake can cost. Suggestions are also given for avoiding common problems, like wrinkled clothing, messy hair, white sock with dark pants, ugly toenail polish, etc.

The whole idea here is to make the client aware of what their responsibilities are. If you don't inform your clients as to what to do and not to do in planning their session, you *deserve* to be sitting in front of your computer every night retouching problems that could easily have been avoided.

In a senior studio, we actually have two clients for each session: the senior themselves and the mother of the senior. Often, the senior makes the appointment and handles planning their session, while the parent's only job to bring the checkbook. Although the senior has usually watched the CD, in most cases the parent has not. To avoid possible problems, we have each parent sign a check-in sheet. This serves as a release for me to use the images in my studio, books, and articles, and also explains the policies of the studio in regard to payments, delivery times, and retouching fees.

Because this is such an important issue, we display posters by each sales area showing what normal retouching covers and additional corrections that can be done and billed to the client. In taking all of these steps to inform our clients, we have greatly reduced the conflicts that can arise from retouching. Most of the time clients will ask, "How much will it be to whiten her teeth?" or "How much will it be to remove that hair?"

Digital correction is no different than any other service you offer in your studio. You have to establish prices that make it profitable, explain to the client how much you charge, and then monitor the actual time you take doing it to avoid reducing your profit.

■ SALES TECHNIQUES

If you offer digital retouching, you need to have a sales presentation rather than producing proofs and leaving them on the counter for the client to pick up (so you don't have to hear it if there is anything they don't like!).

Years ago, I, like many photographers, saw the potential in a sales presentation with proofs produced on transparency material. We had the principal buyers come in and view their session with each pose projected into a 40x60-inch frame. When I first started, this is the only thing that kept my business going. I hated it, because I had to learn how to sell photography, but it taught me how important educating the client was. Sales were amazing, because clients had a professional to help them through the sales process instead of a confusing price list to try to sort out on their own.

As our volume increased to a point that made this type of sales procedure impossible (especially with the number of seniors we photograph), it was challenging to achieve the same level of professional assistance with paper proofs. Then came digital. Once again we had the ability to view images in the studio rather than sending home paper proofs. Now, in fact, each of our clients views their images right after the session is over.

Realizing that informed clients place the largest orders, we begin to educate our clients before they ever come into our studio. When they call to schedule their appointment, the studio person explains the sales process and the convenience of ordering immediately after the session. We have many seniors who travel up to an hour to get to the studio, so the fewer trips the better! The client then prepays their session. Yes, you heard it right *they prepay for the session*. Whenever a client has an question about this procedure, we simply say that we devote several hours to each of our clients with many

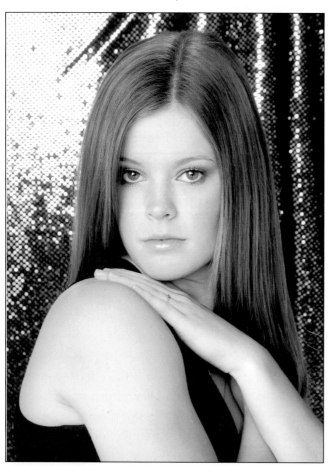

staff members helping them through their session and viewing, so we need to ensure that each session time is scheduled for clients who will be in for their session. We also add that they can cancel up to forty-eight hours before the session and reschedule without additional cost.

At this point, we mail a packet of information to the client. This includes a consultation CD with image effects, music, and voiceovers. In the consultation CD, we ask that the client decide on where in their home they want to display their senior's portraits. Once they decide on that, they use the enclosed colored tissues (provided in various wall-portrait sizes) to determine the appropriate size for the space. Then, we suggest they make out a list of everyone they want to order portraits for. These two things greatly speed up the viewing process. We also discuss normal retouching, which is covered in the image fee, as well as corrections that are sometime necessary to compensate for poor plan-

We are careful to discuss normal retouching, which is covered in the image fee, as well as extra corrections that might need to be made if the client plans poorly (and what these will cost).

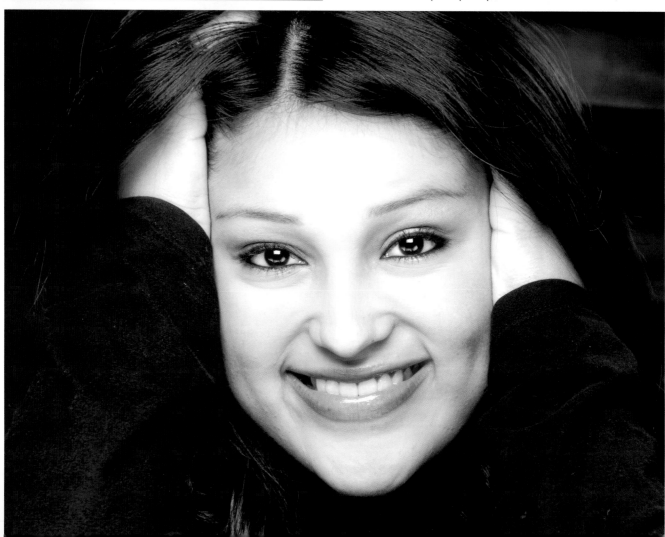

ning (and what the costs are for those jobs). We suggest that if the senior has braces on, wears glasses, or has other problems that may require corrections, that they call the studio so we may try to help them avoid any additional retouching charges.

The client shows up on the day of the session, with the wall-portrait-sized tissue and CD in hand. If they return the CD they receive a credit toward forty additional wallets. We don't actually worry about reusing a twenty-cent CD, but this gives the disc value and makes them more likely to watch it (as well as to buy the additional wallets!).

After the session is over, it takes about fifteen minutes to prepare the images for the viewing session. To fill in this time and further inform our clients, we have another presentation CD set up in a viewing room. This presentation explains the image-selection process, emphasizing that it will be easy and fun. We explain that a trained professional will assist them in picking out the very best pose of each background idea.

The CD also explains retouching, noting that the images they are about to see are not yet retouched, describing what normal retouching is, what images fees are, etc. It also explains all the special effects options like vignettes and black & white. It ends by explaining that the trained assistant will guide the client through all these options.

After they have viewed the CD, the clients are presented with the packages and prices, and an assistant explains the various ways to purchase photographs. The assistant also asks for the wall-portrait-sized tissue so that he or she may direct the client to the packages with the correct size of wall portrait, or show them the area of the price list from which they may add wall portraits to a package in order to design the package that is perfect for them.

By the time our average clients sees their first image, they are very educated. This is why our clients spend as much as they do and why when a pose needs correction they don't argue about who's paying for it.

If digital retouching is requested, we show examples of similar corrections made for other clients (to give the client a realistic expectation). A complete explanation of the process is given and a total time and fee for the correction is written on the slip before the client

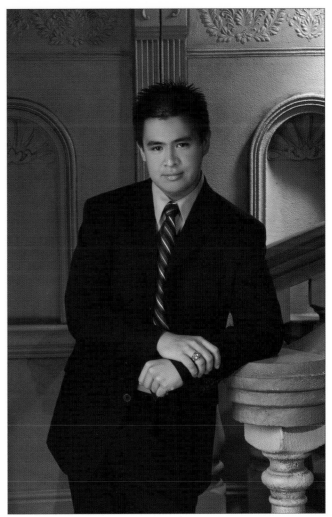

Taking the time to adequately educate your clients is a key factor in creating salable images.

signs it. If the correction is complex, we set up a time for the client to come in and view a test print to ensure they are happy with the correction before we print out the order and complete the correction on all the poses they have ordered.

I can't stress enough the importance of educating your client about the portrait-buying process. I talk with so many photographers who do nothing but complain about their "ridiculous clients." When I ask what they did to educate their client about whatever issue the problem concerned, there is always a long pause or a completely dismissive comment. While this may be *your* thirty-thousandth session, often it is your client's *first*, so teach them how to have a successful experience with your studio.

CHAPTER NINE

DIGITAL FILES

I t doesn't make sense to spend your time correctively lighting and posing a client only to create a digital file that, in and of itself, contains flaws that will have to be corrected to make the image salable. These potentially time-consuming problems include some concerns that are largely unique to digital. For example, with film, who cared about the color of light? It was you lab's job to print out any color cast and match all the skin tones. You could also set your exposure by guess (as long as you were overexposing slightly) and you would end up with a usable image—at least most of the time. I am, of course, exaggerating (well, at least somewhat)—but there was a great deal of latitude when using film. Between the forgiving nature of negative film and the good work of a quality lab, you didn't have to worry about much! Digital is a whole different story.

■ COLOR CONSISTENCY

With digital, the color of light matters—it will change the entire image. Automatic white balance works most of the time, but be prepared for certain colors of clothing and shades of backgrounds to throw off the color across the entire image. In addition, with digital, you

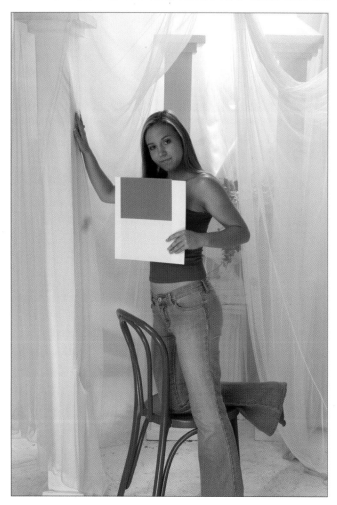

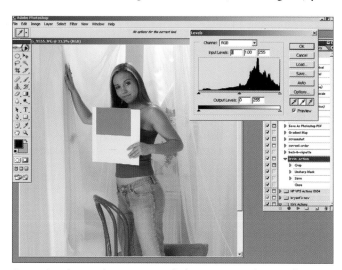

To use Levels to color correct, include a gray or white card in your first shot of any pose where the lighting or lens will change and, in turn, change the color balance. We use a card that is half medium gray and half white. In certain photos, you will find that Photoshop gives a true color with the white card; in others it will be with the gray. These variation are caused by the overall tones and colors of the image.

DIGITAL WORKFLOW

Photographers who grew up with film had an established workflow that safeguarded and stored images from their capture to their delivery. Most of that workflow was handled by an outside lab, so as long as you didn't lose the roll of film or misplace the negatives, you were in good shape. With digital, most of the work in the workflow is now yours. How do you store and safeguard your images, ensure correct filing of the proper images, and retrieve them when it is time to work on the final order?

In our main studio, we have eleven shooting areas and seven camera stations. Each camera is connected to a networked computer. When we shoot an image, the camera downloads the portrait to the media card in the camera and then through the cable to the computer. We use the software that came with our camera to create client files and assign file names to each image. For example, on camera one, we have each file read "cam1," then the camera adds a sequential number. So each file reads "cam1-0001," "cam1-0002," and so on. This saves time when we gather all the images from all the shooting areas. We don't have image numbers that are the same, which often happens without a set prefix. This also gives salespeople a way to explain which setup a particular file is ordered from.

Given our volume, we have one person whose sole job is to sit at a computer burning station, which is networked to all the cameras and sales computers. When a session is complete, one of my assistants hands the person at the burning station the client card with all the background selections listed on the back. This way, he instantly knows which computers will have files of the client on them. He gathers all the camera folders and puts them into one client folder, then burns two CDs of the original images and places them in the client card (which is actually an envelope). After the day's last session, he goes to all the cameras and removes the media cards. He

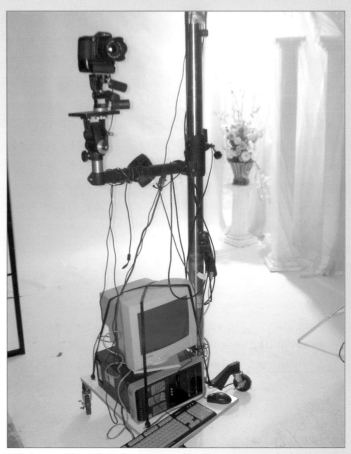

Working with a digital camera tethered to a networked computer allows you to save your images in two locations (to the media card and the computer) and makes it easy to burn a CD of all the images from different camera areas.

then downloads all the images from the cards into a daily backup folder. He burns two copies of this backup and puts them into a file we keep in the studio.

When we photograph outdoors, we go to a separate location rather than a shooting area in back of the studio. I choose locations that have a natural look, so I am often standing on a hillside, in a river, or on rocky cliffs. This is not ideal terrain for lugging along a computer, so we shoot our images only to the media card in the camera. Once the session is over, I have my assistant download the images onto a laptop so the images are stored in two places until we get back to the studio. Then, two CDs are burned of the files stored on the laptop.

With the CD backups made (whether from a studio or location session), the client envelope moves from the burning station to a salesperson. Once the session is viewed, the client's envelope (with CDs, order invoice, and special retouching requirements) is put into production and waits for processing. We track the orders by date and divide them by services needed. We process all orders with 11x14-inch or smaller prints in the studio and send anything 16x20 inches or larger to our lab . Orders that need to be sent to the lab and/or include artwork for client approval are given first priority.

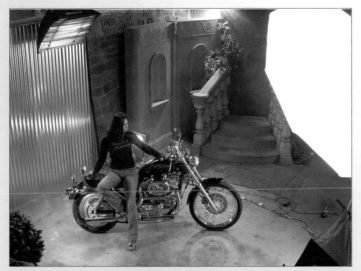

This is one of our largest shooting areas, where the largest props and backgrounds are used. To avoid excessive equipment, the room is designed for the camera, computer, and lighting to work from the center of the room. This avoids major movements and reduces the number of network cables running into the area.

(or someone from your studio) have to make all the skin-tones from a session match. This means if you don't get it captured correctly in the first place, all your profit will be eaten up trying to match inconsistent skin tones.

The first person who helped me as I converted my studios from film to digital told me, "When capturing a digital image for a session, *consistent* color is more important than *good* color!" These are the truest words ever spoken to me on the subject of digital portrait photography. I can enhance poor color and make it salable, but if I have inconsistent color and exposures, I will kill myself trying to match the skin tones to satisfy the client.

Manual white balance is the digital photographer's best friend. White balance your cameras correctly (read your camera manual completely for how to do this) and do it every time you change anything with regard to your lighting or lenses. If you work outdoors using natural light, set the white balance every time you change a scene, because it will affect the color temperature and the overall look of the photograph.

If you have problems with consistency, use a gray or white card to help you match the skin tones from one scene to another, or one style lighting to another. To do this, white balance your digital camera, then take the first photograph of the client in the pose holding gray card or white card in front of them. With a true gray or white card in that first image, you can quickly color balance the images in Photoshop. Simply load the first image of each scene (the one with the grey or white card in front of the subject) and go to Image>Adjustments>Levels.

At the bottom-right corner of the box, you'll see three eyedroppers: one is black, one is gray, and one is white. If you used a gray card, select the grey eyedropper; if you used a white card, select the white eyedropper. Just click on the card with the correct eyedropper and you will see the color adjust to make the card true gray or true white. You can then save these setting for all the images in the series (those with the same lighting setup and scene). This will remove any color casts, but it will not typically give you ideal color for the client's skin tone. The idea here is just to make all your images a consistent color from one background or scene to another. Once you have consistent color throughout the session, then you can adjust the color, contrast, and saturation to achieve good skin color.

■ EXPOSURE

The second friend of the digital photographer is the histogram, a breakdown of your digital image in graph form that shows the tones that make up the captured image. Although most of the time your image won't fill up the entire histogram, for the average scene or setting your exposure needs to be set to fill up at least two-thirds of the histogram for a quality exposure. There are times, in a very low-key or very high-key image, where everything in the image is very dark or very light, that the histogram display will show less-than-normal use of the full tonal range, but that is because of the overall lack of dark or light tones in these images.

All professional digital cameras and most digital cameras for hobbyists have an image information button you can push to quickly see the histogram when setting up your shot. Many photographers set up their camera so that a histogram appears alongside the image preview for each exposure. I prefer not to do this, because it reduces the size of the image in the display and, once the exposure is set properly, I don't *need* to see the histogram; all the images from the same setting will record the same.

As a film guy, when I first started into digital I thought that checking the LCD display gave me all the

---

FILE SIZE

Many photographers purchase cameras or backs that provide more information in each file than they really need. If the largest file size can produce a 40x60-inch print, but you only sell 16x20-inch prints, you need to make a change and stop wasting time with files that are larger than what you actually need. Reduce the size of file your camera is capturing, or sell the camera/back and buy one that will produce up to a 20x24-inch print size (then put the money you saved in the bank)! Cameras are tools, not toys.

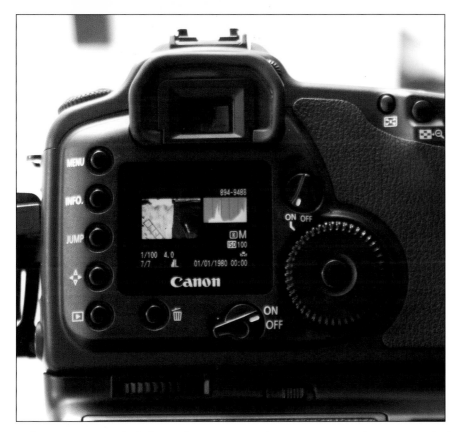

comes to image quality. So, naturally, when I started shooting digital, I shot in the TIFF mode. The file size was huge, the download time was slow, but that provided me the best quality—or so I thought.

One day, the rep from my lab showed me 20x24-inch prints of the same pose captured at three different settings—one as a TIFF, one at the largest (least compressed) JPEG setting, and one at the smallest (most compressed) JPEG setting. At the 20x24-inch size, I saw very little difference between the highly compressed JPEG and the TIFF, but there *was* a slight difference. I saw no difference, however, between the least compressed JPEG and the TIFF.

I told him I wanted to see my own images in the same comparison, so I shot three identical portraits in each of the three file types and sent them to the lab. The results were the same. At that point, I began shooting low-compression JPEGs. This decision was based on the fact that I deal with seniors and, typically, a 20x24-inch is the largest wall portrait they will purchase. If I still photographed families and regularly sold 30x40-inch prints, I would still use the TIFF setting.

Many photographers are absolute quality freaks and, as a result, end up wasting time and money. It goes beyond the *capture* of images—it also involves the storage of images. They believe that files should only be saved as TIFFs or PSDs and with no compression—that way, no quality is lost with opening and closing the same image repeatedly. Of course, repeated saving of compressed files *will* degrade the images. When a file will need to be opened more than once, for additional retouching or other reasons, we save the in-progress file as a TIFF, then save the final file as a JPEG. For the vast majority of our images, however, we open them up, do all the corrections, then save the final files in the JPEG

information I needed about the exposure of my images. Boy, was I wrong! The display is great, but it is so bright that slight variations in exposure can go unnoticed. Additionally, underexposing an image actually makes the skin tones look much richer on the display but doesn't capture the needed information for a quality image. Now, some of you just read that last statement about underexposed images and thought, "But I can fix it!" No you can't—at least not if you want to stay in business, have a life outside of the studio, and make enough money to provide your family with the things they should have.

If you want those things for yourself and your family, you need to get out of the "I can fix anything" mentality right now. When you start using the histogram, setting the manual white balance often, and using gray or white cards, you will be on the right track for producing consistent color for your clients—and you'll start reducing your digital imaging costs.

■ FILE FORMAT

The first decision you must make when you consider workflow is the type of files you are going to capture. I, like most photographers, tend to go overboard when it

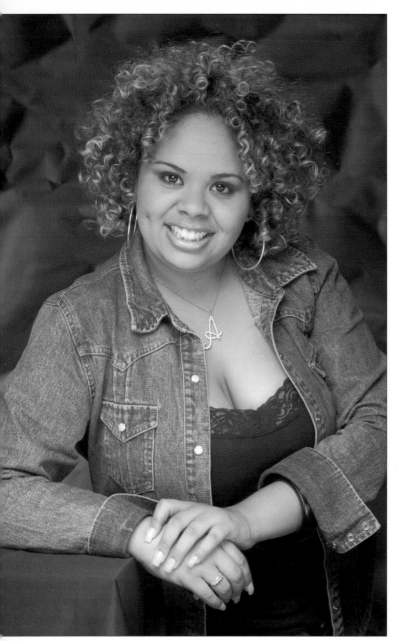

Original portrait.

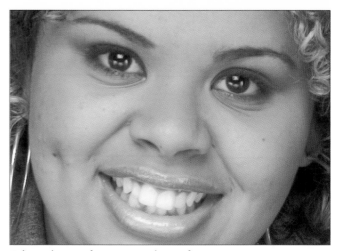

Enlarged view of image saved in TIF format.

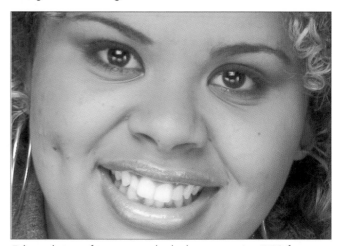

Enlarged view of image saved in high-compression JPEG format.

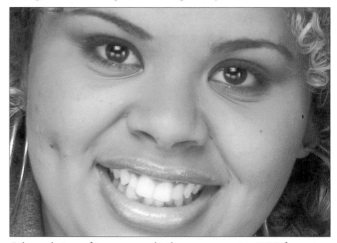

Enlarged view of image saved in low-compression JPEG format.

format. This means our files are only saved twice as JPEGs, once at capture and once for the final order.

Given the extensive quality testing we have done at our largest normal print size, why would I have my employees waste any time saving their work and burning CDs of every file in the larger TIFF format? If there is no difference in quality at my largest print size, why would I fill up my computer storage space and have my machines run slower? The moral to the story is to use a file format that provides you with an adequate result in the shortest amount of time. Time is money, and profit is king!

CHAPTER TEN

NORMAL RETOUCHING

What is "normal" retouching? That has to be determined by you, the photographer, and the expectations of your clients. The first step in retouching an image has nothing to do with Photoshop. As the photographer, it is up to you to determine the look you are going for and then map out the method you want your computer people to use to achieve that look.

■ RETOUCHING STYLE

Just as photographers have a photographic style, people who work in Photoshop have a style of working with an image. That style is based on what looks good to them and the way they learned to do the task at hand. If you have four people working on your images, your images will have four distinct looks in regard to the retouching and corrections that are done. In my studio, I do very little of the computer work on the images from my sessions, but I control the *process* used for all the retouching and corrections. This ensures a uniform look from one session or order to another.

This was a hard lessen to learn, because there are egos involved. When our computer staff first grew to include several new people, I spent a day with each of them demonstrating how I retouched and corrected the most common problems in a senior's image. They all nodded and smiled through the training and said they were impressed with the way our photographs looked. I thought all was well—until the orders started coming out of the lab.

One computer person used the Healing Brush instead of the Clone tool and ended up with dots all over the senior's skin. Another blended the overall skin tone very well but was unobservant when it came to cleaning up all the blemishes. You could easily see that the retouching (and color correction) had been done by different people because there was no continuity.

We started training all over again, except this time I showed my new employees the fruits of their labor and explained why it was unacceptable. I then retouched an image the way I wanted it done, printed it out, and held it up next to theirs. The images not only looked like they had been retouched by different people, they looked like they came from different studios with different photographers!

> It is up to you to determine the look you are going for and map out the method you want your computer people to use.

There were two retouchers who knew much more about computers than I did—one of them was older and one was younger. The younger of the two saw the difference in quality, realized the validity of what I was saying, and currently runs my studio's lab. The older gentleman explained why he preferred his way of working in Photoshop and that, in all his experience, his was the best way to retouch an image. After he finished, I explained that I only know how to do three things on a computer: make money, find the fastest way to accomplish what needs to be done, and achieve the look I want my photographs to have. Beyond that, I don't care how it works or what else it can do. Needless to say, he is no longer employed by our studios.

The method of retouching you will use is the most important process to establish, because it is done on each and every image ordered. If you can't master this, you will constantly send out work that has no distinct style or look. This sounds very complex, but it isn't. Simply make notes on each step you take and the tools you use to get an image ready to send to the printer. This gives your employees a step-by-step guide to follow to ensure consistency.

The look I want for my seniors is smooth skin with no blemishes, blotchiness, or shine. I want the darkness under the eyes eliminated and the darkness on each side of the bridge of the nose lessened. I feel the eyes must "pop," so I want both the main and secondary catchlights enhanced to draw the eye of the viewer to the eyes in the portrait. I like a more glamorous look in my images, which is reflected in my style of retouching.

It is my job to outline for each computer person the specific steps, tools, and settings I use to obtain the look that I am going for. If they don't produce that look, it is not their fault—it's mine.

■ OUR PROCESS

The following is a detailed description of the procedures we use to achieve the look I want. You may use different tools, different settings, and have different methods to obtain your studio's standardized retouching—and that's fine as long as you have a standardized retouching process for your studio.

Retouching the Subject. After the image is opened, we color correct the image, because adjustments to the contrast, saturation, and color will change the appearance of the skin.

Once color correction is done, we look at the print size that is being ordered from the pose being retouched. The final size will dictate how much retouching is done. If only wallets are ordered from a full-length pose, very little retouching will be necessary. If, however, the client has ordered a 20x24-inch print of a head-and-shoulders shot, the image will require more extensive retouching to achieve the same look.

We instruct our computer people to retouch the image about two to three times larger on the screen than the largest print size that will be made from the file. If you are retouching for wallets, the image on the screen should be a 4x5- to 5x7-inch size. If you are retouching for an 8x10-inch print, the image should be 11x14 to 16x20 inches on the screen. Of course, these dimensions are just approximate. The point is to keep your computer people from over-retouching, which wastes time and money. If you don't see this as a problem, go in and watch people retouching. Whether the final output size is a wallet or 30x40-inch print, they will have the image magnified to see just the eye and part of the nose on the monitor. This wastes a huge amount of time. Retouching by size keeps your orders moving as quickly as possible.

When retouching, we start off with the Clone Stamp tool set at 23-percent opacity. Why 23 percent? I like it better than 22 or 24, to be honest—but as long as it's in this area, it really doesn't matter (now 33 percent *would* matter). We start at the top of the face and work down. Typically, we start off with the skin between and slightly above the eyebrows. It is a middle-tone skin color and is good for lightening the darker areas and darkening the shiny areas.

Rather than trying to remove individual blemishes, I like using a large, soft-edged brush to blend large areas of skin. We select the Clone Stamp, press Opt/Alt, and click to sample the area to be cloned. While holding down the left mouse button, I start making sweeping motions across the skin. For general smoothing, one sweep is enough. For problem areas that have shine or bad texture, multiple passes are needed to blend away the problem.

I look at retouching as a way to correct flaws both in the client but also in the photographic process. There are differences between shooting digital and film. Despite all the benefits that digital has, it also has shortcomings. Digital doesn't work well with oily skin that reflects light. Shadow areas also tend to pick up colors other than the skin tone, getting darker and darker as the shadow recedes to near black. Even when the subject has a beautiful skin tone, the shadows will often have a greenish appearance, and normal shine on the skin will often glow. These are problems that need to be corrected. A simple swipe from the Clone Stamp tool and the greenish cast is lessened by adding in skin color. Because we use a lower opacity, the shadow isn't drastically lightened.

There are other shadow areas and areas of the skin that can appear too dark and need to be corrected, as well. These are the shadows on each side of the bridge of the nose and under the bottom lip (with a subject with full lips). You may also need to adjust the skin color all around the mouth and chin. Since the main light is closer to the top of the face than the bottom, the skin in this area often appears slightly darker and needs to be lightened to match the rest of the face.

Once I've retouched the entire face with a large brush, I go back to any areas that need a different size brush and more or less opacity. Once the skin is smooth, the blemishes eliminated, and the shadows corrected, I then move on to the eyes.

To enhance the eyes, I use the Dodge tool, setting it to 50 percent and Highlights in the options bar at the top of the screen. I select a soft-edged brush that is approximately the size of the main catchlights. I posi-

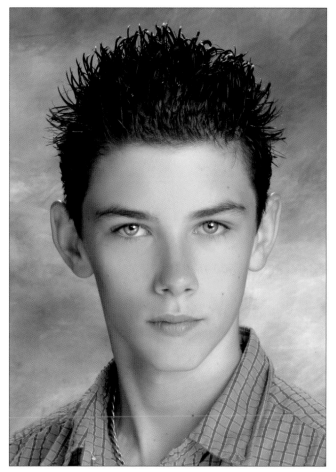

Every client image needs to receive standard retouching using the same tools and steps to the same level of correction. We start off using the Clone Stamp tool to blend the skin. Once the problem areas are softened, we correct any shadows areas that are too heavy or off color. The final step is to enhance the catchlights with the Dodge tool. We count the number of clicks on the first eye and then duplicate them on the second eye to avoid a noticeable difference between the catchlights.

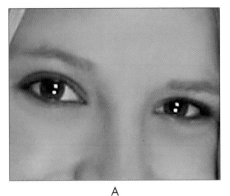

A

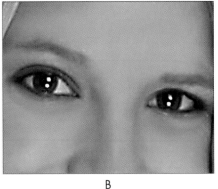

B

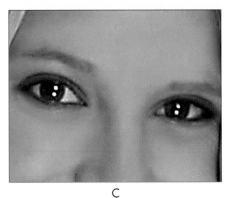

C

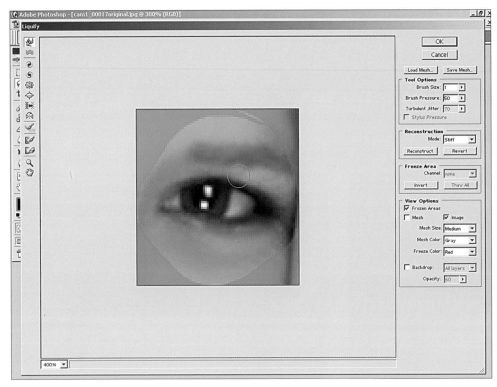

Most of the time, you can make uneven eyes look the same size by matching the catchlights in the eyes. Even though the opening of each eye will still be a different size, if the catchlights look identical, the problem will be less visible. If this doesn't work (A), the next option is to use the Liquify filter (shown to the left) to enlarge the smaller eye. As you do this, you may notice that it distorts the upper or lower lid of the eye (B). If this happens, use an area from the uncorrected eye to replace what has been distorted (C).

tion the brush over the first catchlight and count the number of clicks needed to make the catchlight as bright as I want it. I then go to the other eye and repeat the same number of clicks over the second main catchlight. This way they appear to have the same brightness.

You can use the same process when a client has one eye that appears to be smaller than the other. Typically, the reason the eye seems smaller is that you see more of the main catchlight in the larger eye; in the smaller eye, some of the catchlight is usually hidden by the top eyelid. If you enlarge the catchlight in the smaller eye to match the size and brightness of the catchlight in the larger eye, both eyes seem to be the same size.

This is the extent of retouching that comes with our normal retouching fee. Any other retouching is billed to the client and falls into the "extensive" re-touching category, which is offered to the client with a quote sheet.

At this point I need to say, again, that there are many ways to accomplish the same task. Some photographers like the Healing Brush, some work with the Patch tool. I have tried them and I found they worked well but didn't give me the look I wanted. I found the Healing Brush often created a spotty appearance (although if I had one enormous zit to retouch quickly, that would be my tool of choice). The Patch tool is great for retouching skin, but I find it slower for me (and my computer people) to work with. Time is money, so I use the Clone Stamp tool.

Retouching the Background. After the subject is completely retouched, I look at the entire image to see if there are any flaws in the background/floor. We are a high-volume studio, so our white floor and sets get marks on them throughout the day. This is not something I want my clients to see.

A standard correction for any pose on the white floor is done using the Lasso tool. I adjust the feather

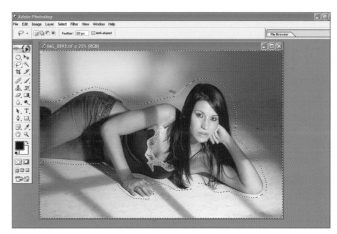

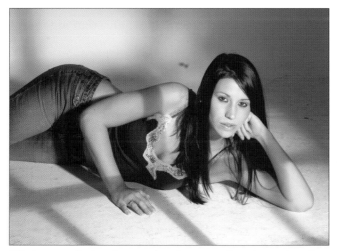

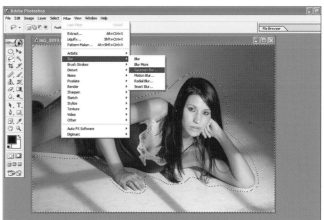

Working in a high-volume studio, the issue of marks on the white floor in the high-key areas (above) has been an ongoing battle. In the summer, which is our busiest time, we paint the white floor each night after sessions and the marks return halfway through the next day because of the amount of traffic. To hide these marks, we select the area (top right) and use the Gaussian Blur filter (right).

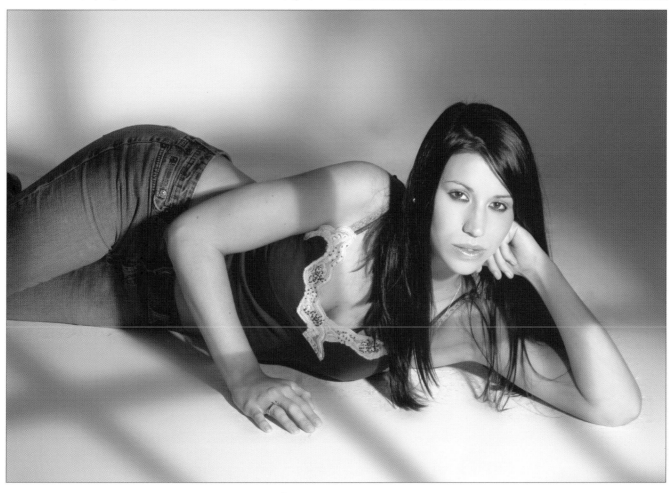

setting (in the options bar) to at least 30 pixels, then use the Lasso tool to rope off the floor area. If the entire floor and background is white, I simply rope off the subject, right mouse click, and choose Select Inverse from the drop-down menu. This selects the entire image other than the subject. Then I select Filter>Blur>Gaussian Blur and adjust the blur to eliminate any marks on the background. To eliminate any simple marks on the set or background, I use the Clone Stamp tool.

Vignetting. Once the retouching is complete, the final step is to add a vignette to the image if it is requested. A vignette simply makes the image darker, lighter, or blurrier around the edges. Many painters use this darkening of the edges around the point of focus as a way to hold the viewer's attention where it should be.

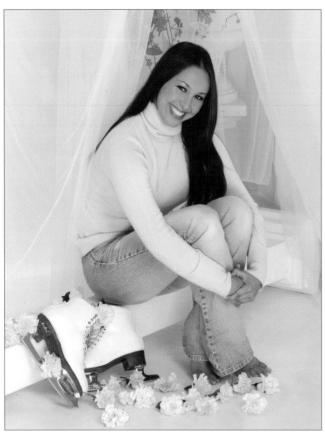

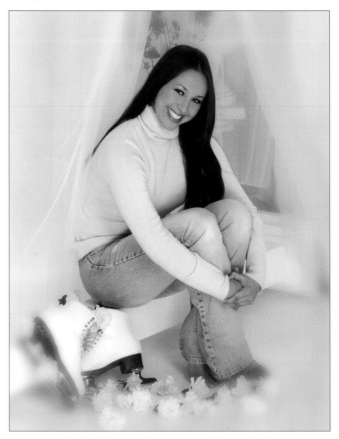

Vignettes are used to hold the viewer's attention on the subject by reducing or eliminating lines that lead out of the frame. With film, you would use a vignetter on the camera; with digital, you just add a vignette before the image goes to the printer. I normally use the Marquee tool to select an oval area (right), then feather the selection to 200 pixels for a blended look. I inverse the selection, and then use the Brightness/Contrast command to darken (or lighten) it. I often blur the area as well, as seen in the final image (top right).

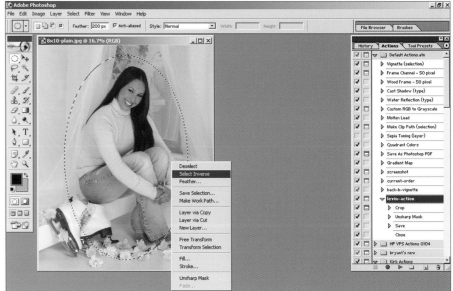

There are no rules to follow when it comes to vignettes. Some photographers use them around the entire image, some just at the bottom of the frame. I have examples of the vignettes we offer in the sales areas, and I have the salespeople suggest the appropriate vignette for the image (or the client can choose not to have a vignette—the choice is theirs).

The process of preparing the image for the vignette is the same whether you darken, lighten, or blur the selected area. For a complete vignette, select the Elliptical Marquee tool, set the feather amount to 200 pixels, then click and drag over the focal point of your image to select an oval area of the height and width you feel is appropriate. At this point, right mouse click and choose Select Inverse, which will select everything outside of the subject area. At this point, you are ready to create your vignette. If the portrait is low key (darker background), go to Image>Adjustments>Brightness/Contrast. Reduce the brightness to create the desired effect. If the image is high key (light background), follow the exact same steps but lighten the selected area until you get the desired effect. I seldom use a white vignette. I prefer to blur the selected areas of high-key portraits. This adds a dreamy look, rather than just turning edges white, and can be done using the Gaussian Blur filter.

For a vignette on the bottom of the image only, the process is similar, just use a different tool. Select the Lasso tool and draw a U-shaped selection around the feet and off to the sides of the image, then continue the selection along the outer edges of the bottom and sides of the image. Once the selected area is where you what it, simply use the above methods to darken, lighten, or blur the area for the desired result.

Converting to Black & White. We have one more step in finishing the average order. Many clients like the look of black &

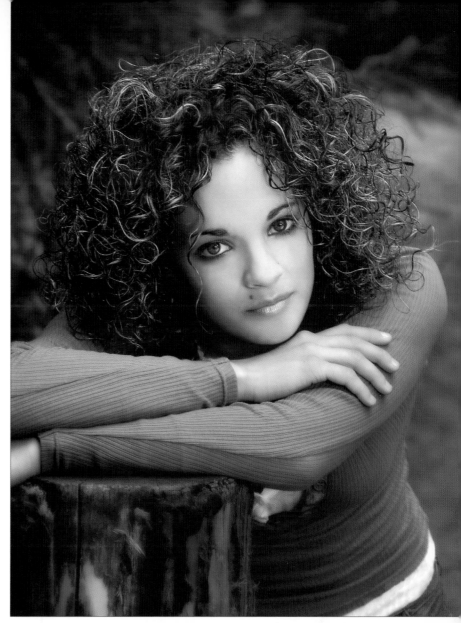

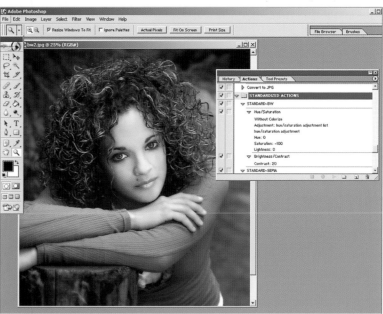

When creating black & white images, using an action ensures consistent results.

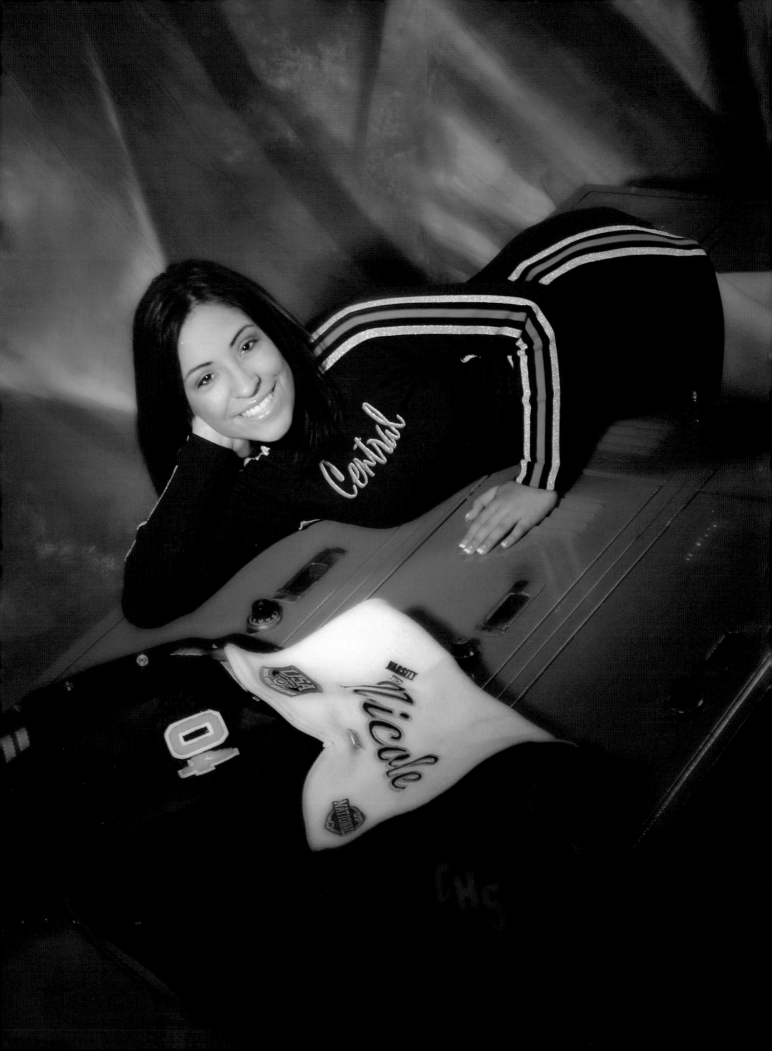

white, so we need to convert color digital files to black & white images. This is a really simple thing that photographers have tried, with all their might, to complicate. I have seen actions that involve fifteen steps! Again time is money, so if you have a favorite method for converting images to black & white and it is saved as an action, that's great. We produce many beautiful black & white images with a two-step process. We desaturate the image (Image>Adjustments>Desaturate), which takes the color out of the image, while leaving the image in RGB mode. At this point the photograph will appear flat and lack contrast. We simply boost the contrast by 10 points (Image>Adjustments>Brightness/Contrast) and we have a beautiful black & white image. If you want to add a warm tone, add red and yellow to the black & white image, but again, put it into an action and make it standardized so everyone's color is the same. For more on actions, see pages 111–14.

That's it! Now the vast majority of your clients' orders are ready to go to the printer. You have profited because you have been paid for your time spent correcting the images, and your clients are happy because they look great. Next, we will start discussing ways to correct problems created by the client (which they will pay for), as well as the photographer (which you will pay for).

As seen on the facing page, the Move is an action that vignettes and softens the edges of an image—instantly!

CHAPTER ELEVEN

OTHER COMMON CORRECTIONS

All that we have discussed leading up to this point has dealt with getting the average original image out of the camera and preparing it for the printer. You have done your job in the camera room, the client has done their job preparing for the session—life is good. Now, we will start to discuss the most common corrections that are needed when things don't work out as they should. Sadly, the most common corrections for the average photographer don't have anything to do with the client but are caused by the photographer himself.

■ POOR FOCUS

I started into photography when everyone used Hasselblads, Mamiyas, or Bronicas. Everyone had bright screens that aided their focus, until their eyes went bad and they had to rely on corrective optics for the finder. The first autofocus cameras were like a godsend! Finally, we could relax and not have to focus back

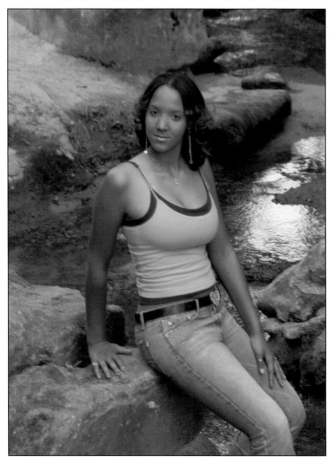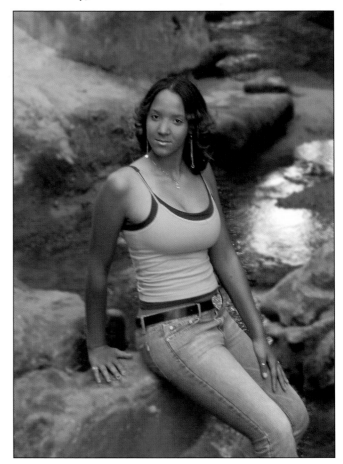

If an image is slightly lacking in sharpness (left), digital sharpening filters can improve the situation (right).

You must fix any focus problems before the client sees an image. If you don't, the image will never be clear enough; the client will always be looking for signs of the shot being out of focus.

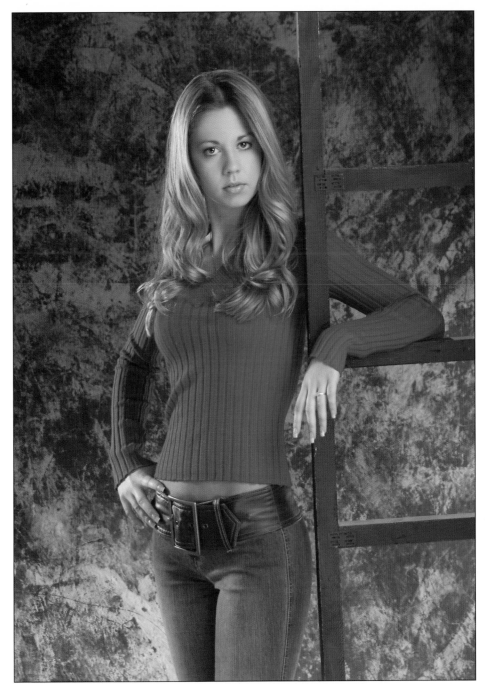

and forth until the image was crystal clear. I have been using autofocus cameras for the last seven years and I love it—except when they don't focus on the area I want in focus.

More often than many young portrait photographers think, even a quality autofocus camera will actually focus on a point other than where it originally focused. We all get a little lazy or distracted from time to time and end up concentrating on the session while letting the camera worry about focus. This leads to a serious situation when the client's favorite image is the one in which the autofocus decided to focus on the rock beside Dad's head, instead of on Dad's face.

You have to realize that no matter *how* good a sharpening tool you use, there are many photographs that are simply too out of focus to be fixed. The second thing to remember is you must fix any focus problems or eliminate the out-of-focus pose *before the client sees it!* If you let a client see a soft image and then try to fix it, it will never be clear enough; they will always be looking for signs of the shot being out of focus.

Basic sharpening of an image is a two-step process. First, you need to bring detail to the area that should be in focus. Next, you need to eliminate sharp detail from the mistaken point of focus in the background or foreground.

Let me explain. Most photographers confronted with a problem of unwanted softness go to their favorite sharpening tool: Unsharp Mask (Filter>Sharpen>Unsharp Mask). They adjust the amount of sharpening to be able to see detail in the subject. The problem is, they have also proportionately increased detail in the area that was *already* in focus. So even though the client does now have some detail in their eyes and clothing, the rock, tree, or painted background still has a great deal *more* detail because it has been sharpened, too. Therefore, your eyes still see the subject as soft.

The easiest way to approach this problem is to select the in-focus area with your Lasso tool, then blur it with the Gaussian Blur filter (Filter>Blur>Gaussian Blur) to a point that it appears more out of focus than your subject. Also, look for any other elements in the photograph that have more detail than the subject and soften them, too. Once the subject is the sharpest point in the image, use your favorite sharpening tool to increase the detail on the subject. For extremely soft images, you may want to select just the subject to sharpen. In either case, look to create adequate detail on the subject without giving the image an unappealing oversharpened look. If you can't accomplish this, trash the image before the client sees it.

The eyes are the window to the soul; if they appear to have detail, the rest of the portrait will too. There-fore, the final step is to enlarge the image on screen to view just the eyes. Start by defining the catchlights as we discussed previously. You will then define the distinct lines of and around the eye. How you work will depend on the size of the image—whether it's a head-and-shoulders shot, full-length, etc. If the photo is a close-up, you can define the line around the color portion of the eye as well as the eyelashes. In a full-length photo, defining the catchlights is about all you can do without making the photograph appear unnatural.

If you have a second image that is almost the same but sharper, you can, as a last resort, place the soft image on a new layer over the sharp one. Then you can erase the eyes, hair, and eyebrow area of the soft image to reveal the more detailed versions of these areas in the underlying image.

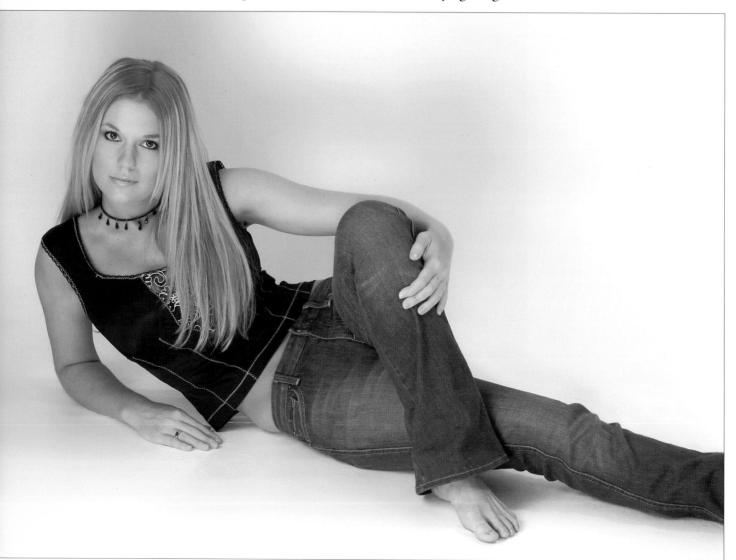

In portraits, the critical areas of focus are the eyes and lips.

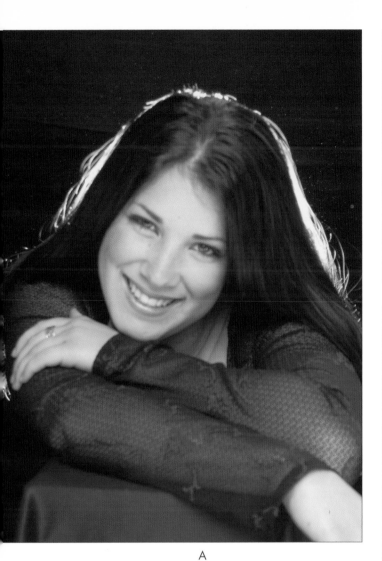

A

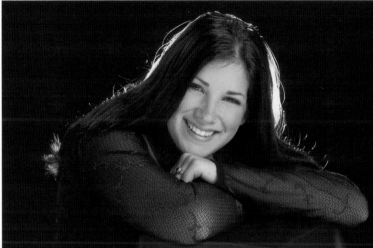

B

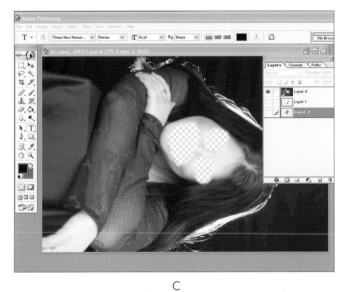

C

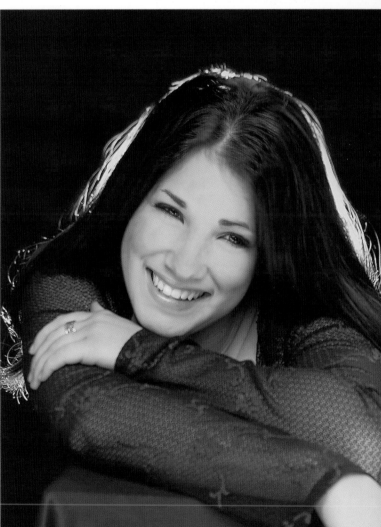

D

Occasional focus problems are a fact of life (A). If you have a second image that is almost the same but sharper (B), you can place the soft image on a new layer over the sharp one. Then you can erase the eyes, hair, and eyebrow area of the soft image (C) to reveal the more detailed versions of these areas in the underlying image (D).

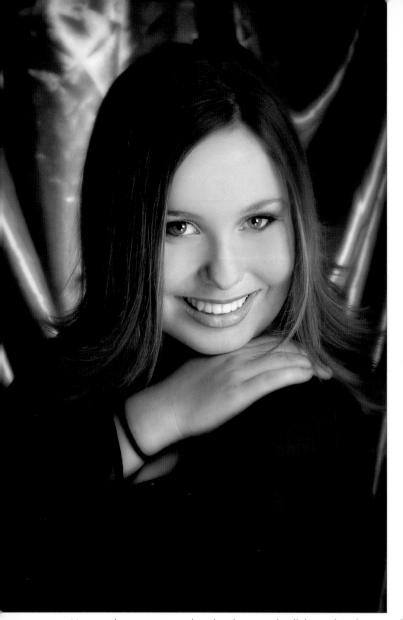
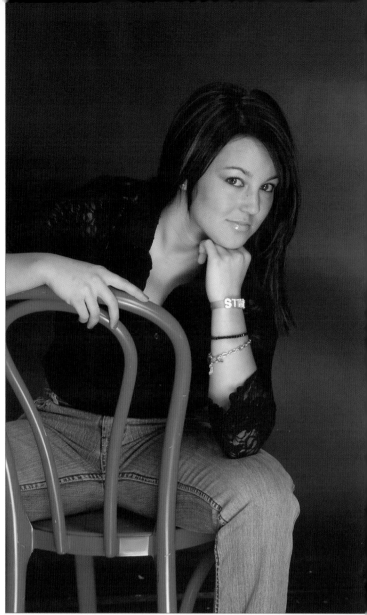

How much a portrait needs to be sharpened will depend on the size of the subject's face within the frame and the size of the prints that will be made from the file.

This only works well, of course, if you used a tripod or camera stand to create the portraits; if you handheld your camera, the images won't line up perfectly. In an area of the studio where we handhold the cameras, we recently had an autofocus lens that would indicate it was focused when it actually wasn't (it was close, but not perfect). Luckily, the lens died completely within a day of when this problem started. Another lucky break was that most of the orders for the images shot with this lens happened to be for small prints where the problem wasn't apparent. There was, however, one order from a client who wanted an 11x14-inch print. Since all of the images from this camera were soft, we found a similar pose taken with a different camera in another camera area. We duplicated the sharp eyes, hair,

and eyebrows and blended them onto the soft image. The final portrait made the client happy and saved the embarrassment of having to reshoot the image (which would have been really difficult, since the senior had since cut her hair).

If none of these steps make the image appear focused, the image is not salvageable. You can spend the next few hours of your life trying to breathe life back into the image, but is it really worth it? The answer will be found in how many other poses were taken and if it is possible to reshoot the image.

■ POOR COMPOSITION

Another common photographer-caused problem comes from composing an image through a viewfinder that isn't formatted to the final composition of the images we must print out. If you shoot your digital images with a 35mm-style camera, the final output size should be 8x12 inches, not 8x10 inches. If you think this problem will be remedied anytime soon, ask a photographer who shoots weddings with a Hasselblad how the 5x5-inch frame market is nowadays. (Hasselblad and some other medium-format cameras use a 2¼-inch square negative, thereby producing 5x5- not 4x5-inch proofs.)

In composing an image in a viewfinder that isn't formatted to the final composition size, we have two problems to consider. First, if we leave *too much* extra room on the top and bottom of the image to compen-

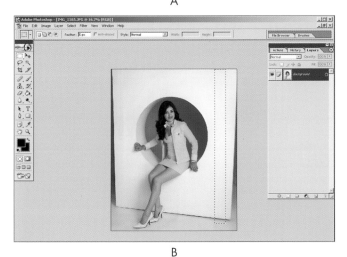

A

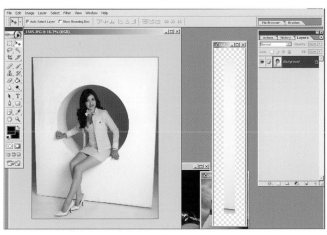

B

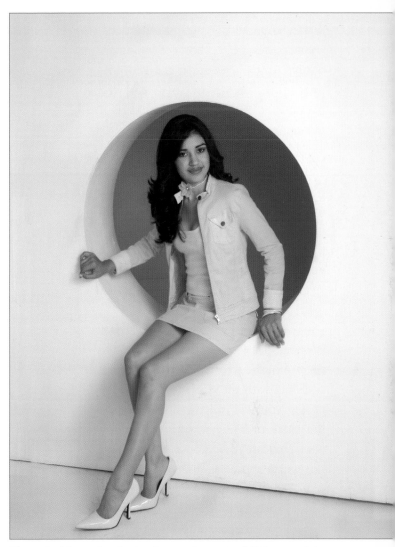

The end of the wall on both sides is a distraction (A). To extend the background, simply use the Marquee tool to select a strip of the existing background that is wider and taller than the area that needs to be extended (B). Copy this area onto a new image canvas (C), then drag the strip of the background back to the original image to fill in the area. For this particular photo, we then repeated the process on the left side to match the shade of white as it varies from one side to the other (above).

C

sate for this difference, we waste our image quality by using only a portion of the file. If we leave *too little* space to compensate for this problem, we end up cropping off the tops of our clients' heads or their feet. No matter how careful you are, at some point you will end up composing a photograph closer than you should. When this happens, your choices are to chop off some part of the client's body at the top and bottom of the frame, or to extend the background at the sides of the image to fit the print size.

This is one time *not* to use the Clone Stamp tool. This tool duplicates the pattern of the background too well, revealing the fact that the background has been duplicated. The easiest way to fix this problem is to open the original image and duplicate the background layer (Layer>Duplicate Layer) giving yourself a copy to work on. Then, crop your image to the size you want it (set the height at width in the options bar at the top of the screen). As you first click and drag with the Crop tool over your image, you will only be able to go to the sides of the photograph. At this point, release the mouse button and boxes will appear at the corners of the crop box. Click and drag on these to extend the cropping indicator past the sides of the image, composing the portrait with enough room at the top and bottom of the image. Then, hit Return to crop the image.

At this point, empty white space will appear on each side of your image.

Making sure that every aspect of the portrait looks just right is critical to salable images. This includes making smart decisions when planning and shooting the session, as well as when retouching the images to eliminate any remaining problems with the subject's appearance.

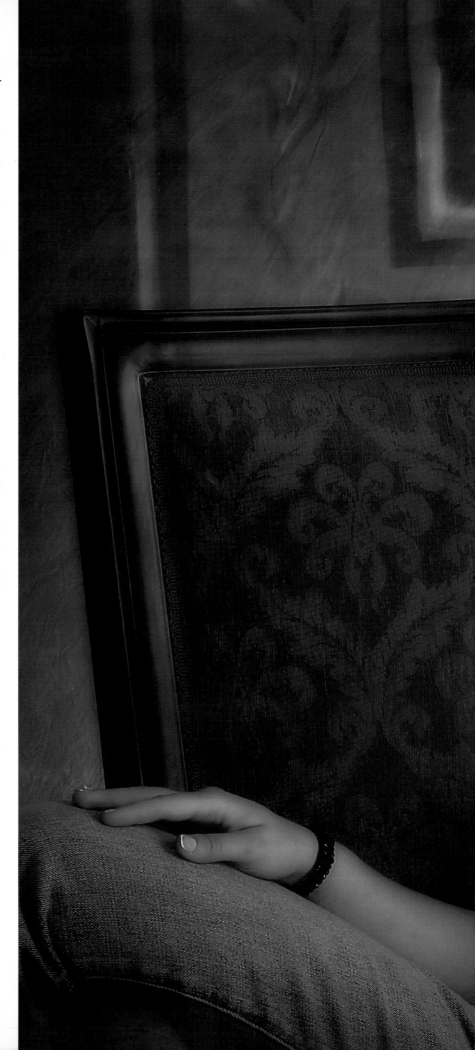

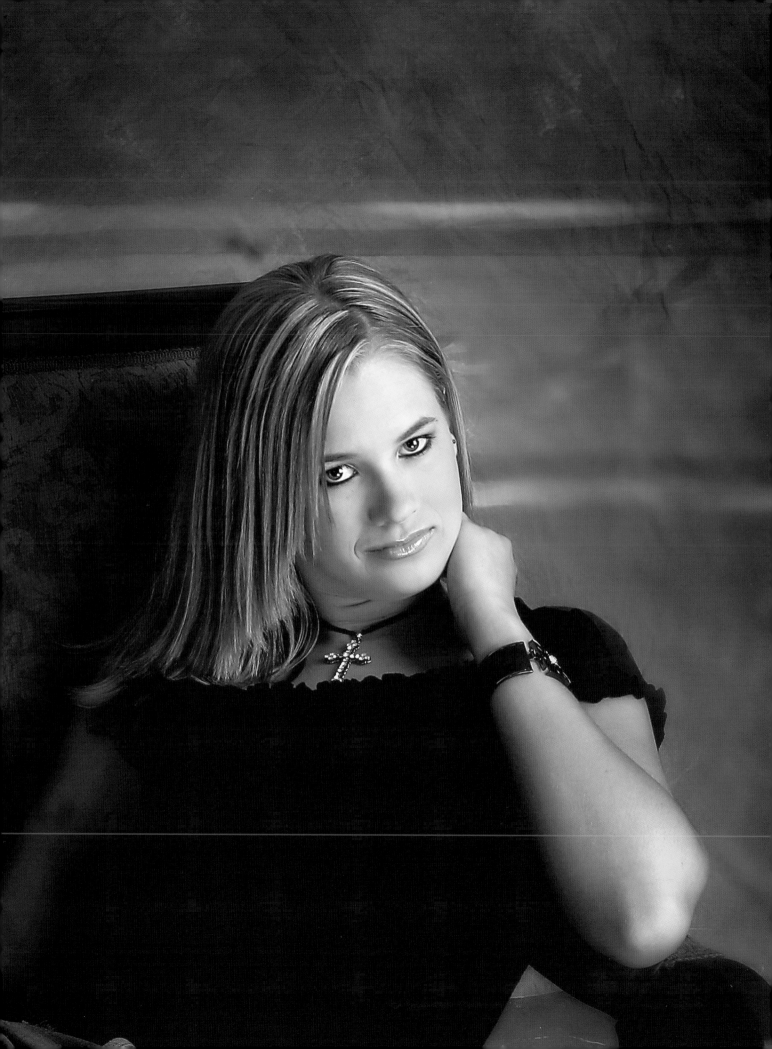

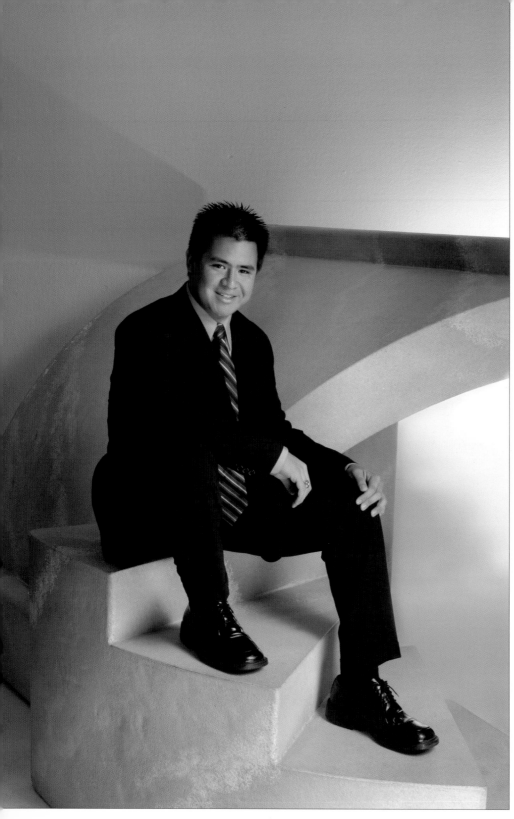

cropped image into your new blank canvas on three separate layers. Center the top layer, then move one underlying layer to the left and one to the right, filling in the blank space with the background. You may need to do some cleanup with the Clone Stamp tool, but it is much better than cutting off body parts.

■ POOR EXPOSURE

The next correction is one that all digital photographers hate to make. When you picked up your first digital camera the big warning you probably received was, "Whatever you do, don't overexpose your images!" Sooner or later, though, you'll be faced with images that are overexposed and that you can't reshoot . . . and you'll be just about ready to lay an egg! I will be the first to tell you, this correction isn't a flawless one—it isn't going to make the image look as good as it would have if you had exposed it properly—but with a little work, it may save your bacon.

This correction multiplies layers to build back the detail that was lost due to overexposure. There is a limit to the amount of overexposure this will fix, but it

In the options bar, delete your settings from the width, height, and resolution fields so nothing appears in those boxes. Then, crop the white borders off your image. This gives you an image that is the correct final height but narrower than the standard size. Now, create a new file that is the final size and resolution you intend your photograph to be (File>New). Copy the can help. The first step is to use the Clone Stamp tool to reduce as much as possible any glowing highlights on the face. The success of this will be determined by the amount of overexposure. Once the glow is minimized, create a duplicate layer on top of the original. Open the layers palette and set the mode of the overlying layer to Multiply. Next, duplicate another layer on top of the image. You will notice it appears darker. If it is too dark, reduce the layer's opacity. If the image still appears overexposed, duplicate another layer.

As the layers build, you will notice the contrast increasing in the portrait. Once you are done adding layers, you can fix this by reducing the contrast of the photograph (Image>Adjustments>Brightness/Contrast). Once the contrast is adjusted, flatten the image and use the Clone Stamp tool to conceal any highlights that are still blown out.

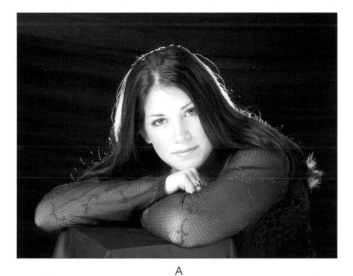

A

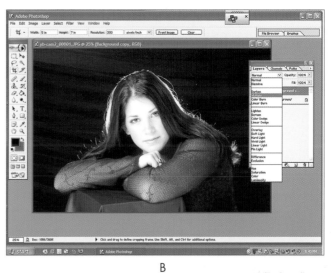

B

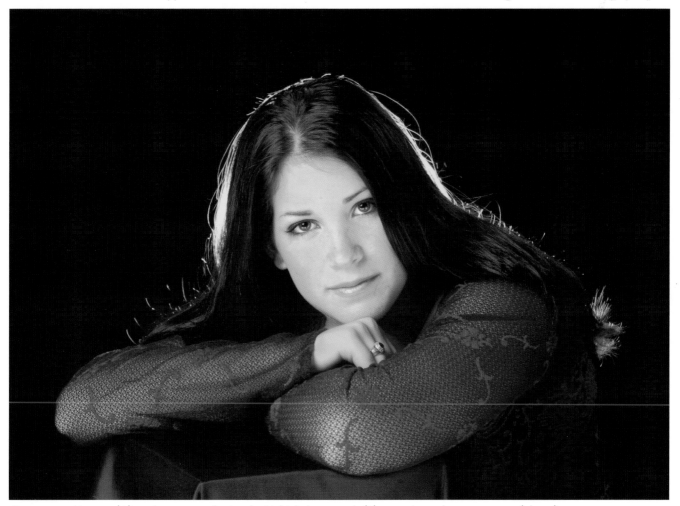

Overexposed images (A) can be corrected using the Multiply layer mode (B) to produce a better exposure (above).

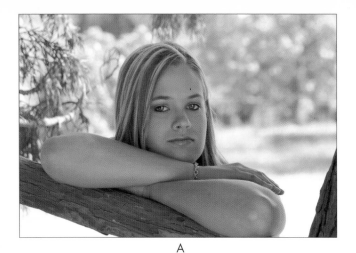

A

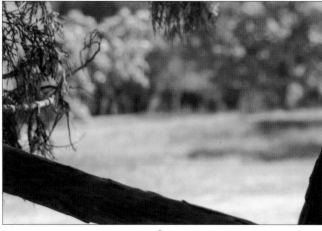

B

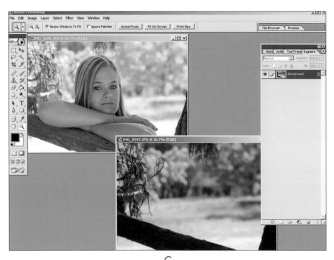

C

I work at outdoor locations throughout the day. This means that backgrounds can have hot spots or areas that, when the subject is placed in shade, will be in direct sun and appear much too bright for the exposure set for the subject (A). To ensure this isn't a problem, I photograph the subject. Then, when the subject leaves, I take one more shot using the exact same composition, but without the subject and with the exposure set for the brightness of the background (B). I do this for each background that I worry will be too light because of direct sun. Then, in Photoshop, I place the portrait on a layer over the background-only image and erase the light background area from the top image to reveal the darker foliage underneath (C). When this is completed, the result in an image in which the exposure on both the subject and the background is correct (below).

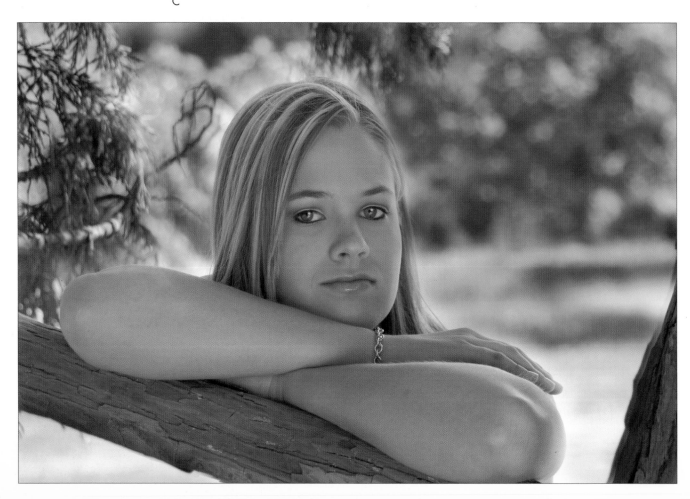

■ BACKGROUND PROBLEMS

Another good example of the use of layers is found when taking outdoor photographs. At my studio, we set up an entire day of outdoor appointments for a single location, so we have to deal with lighting as it changes throughout the day. Wedding photographers find themselves in the same situation. How many times do you go to an outdoor location to create a portrait, place the subject in shade, and find that at least some of the background is in bright sun? With the shaded subject correctly exposed, the areas of the background that are in direct sun are blown out. To combat this, after the last shot of the subject, I have the client step out of the scene and I take a shot of the background, metering for the sunlit areas. I do this with each pose. When a pose with a blown-out area is ordered, I simply open the image without the subject (the one metered for the sunlight) then place the ordered image (with the blown-out background) on a layer above it. Using the Eraser tool, I re-

move the blown-out areas, revealing the properly exposed image data on the underlying layer.

We back up our school-dance and prom backgrounds in the same way. Once the background is set

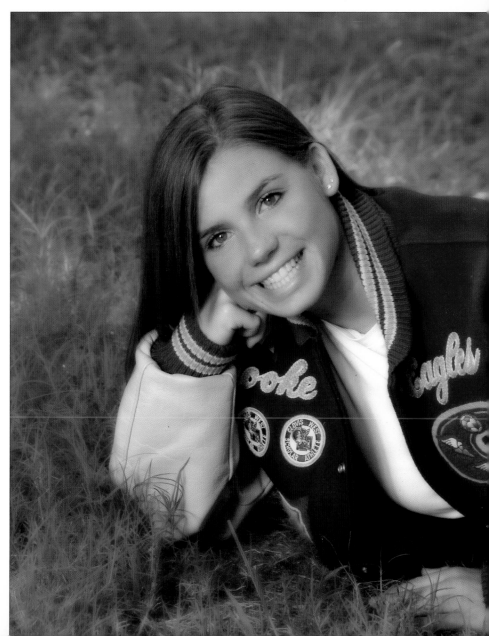

While you can *fix your outdoor backgrounds digitally using Adobe Photoshop, remember that working in a carefully selected location that doesn't* require *you to do so will save both time and money.*

up and tested, we photograph the first image of the background only. If a gel falls off the light or a background light stops working and our photographer doesn't catch it, we digitally replace the problem area of the background with the first image without a couple.

■ WHITENING THE TEETH

Now, we move on to the most frequently used digital corrections to address problems with the client. Most corrections will obviously be done to the head and face, because this area is in each and every portrait you take. Probably the most common enhancement we are asked for is for the teeth to be whitened. This simple correction is billed to the client. The average quote is for fifteen minutes. The correction usually takes less than five minutes, but we have the extra time if needed.

To whiten the teeth, you simply select the entire area of the teeth using the Lasso tool. Once the entire area is selected, brighten the teeth using the Brightness/ Contrast command. How dark the teeth appear will determine how much you will lighten them and increase the contrast. The basic rule of correction is to under-correct rather than over-correct! Once the teeth appear slightly brighter, but not noticeably bright, color correct them. Usually, teeth have a yellowish color, which means you will typically add blue to the selected area to make them appear whiter.

Probably the most requested correction in portrait photography is to whiten the subject's teeth (A). To do this, use the Lasso tool to select the teeth (B). Then, add blue to the teeth to make them less yellow (Image>Adjustments>Color Balance). Finally, lighten the teeth to make them brighter (but not pure white—overdoing it will create a unnatural look). Once the color and brightness of the teeth are to your liking, select the Clone Stamp tool to clean up the dark areas on and between the teeth (C).

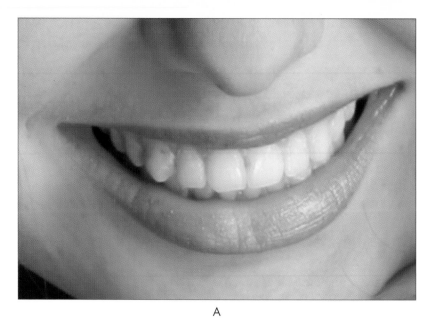

A

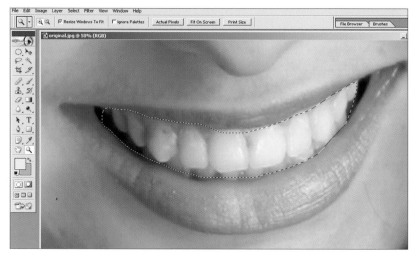

B

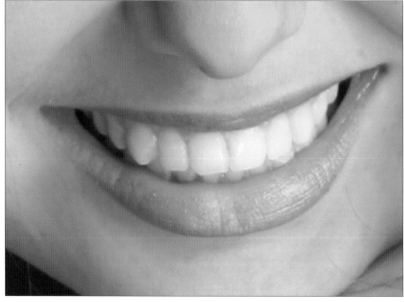

C

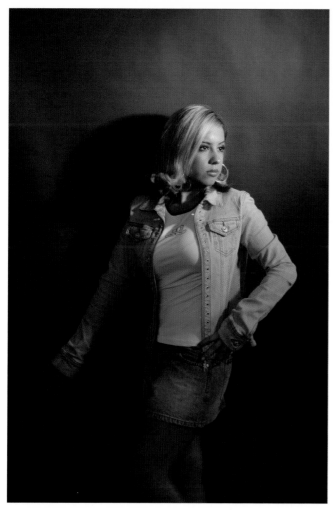

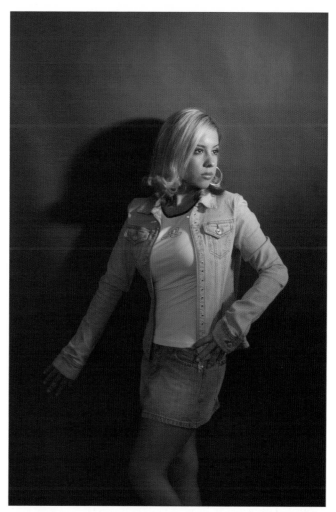

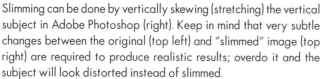

Slimming can be done by vertically skewing (stretching) the vertical subject in Adobe Photoshop (right). Keep in mind that very subtle changes between the original (top left) and "slimmed" image (top right) are required to produce realistic results; overdo it and the subject will look distorted instead of slimmed.

After you have the teeth looking more presentable, then you can select the Clone Stamp tool, at a low opacity, and use it to lighten the dark areas that appear between the teeth.

■ SLIMMING THE SUBJECT

Some photographers skew their portraits, elongating them to make their clients appear thinner. Here again you risk changing the appearance of the subject to correct a problem. If you want to try this, open an image and go to Edit>Free Transform. A line will appear around the photo, with small boxes on all four sides as well as at the four corners. To elongate the image, just put the cursor on the center box at the top of the photograph and drag it slowly upward. A little move goes a

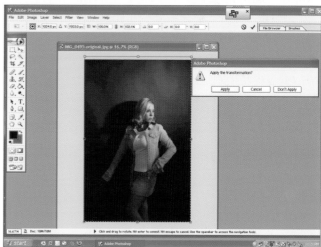

long way. Once you are done stretching Aunt Betty, click on the image and select Apply or Cancel, depending on whether or not you like the results. You should only try this if the client is standing with their body and arms positioned vertically in the frame. If the arms or legs run horizontally, stretching the image will just increase their size!

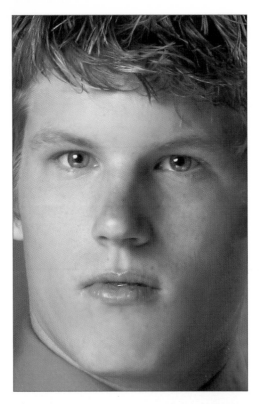

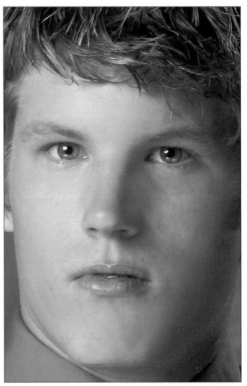

While shadows are our friends when hiding flaws, they can also create problems on the face. The shadow on the side of the nose often needs to be softened to avoid drawing attention to the size of the nose. A shadow that is too prominent can also make the eye socket appear deeper on the shadow side of the face than on the highlight side. With digital, shadows often have a color (often greenish) instead of being a gradual transition of skin color from the highlight to the darkest shadow. To correct any shadow, simply use the Clone Stamp tool, set to a low opacity, to blend in a natural skin color while lightening the shadow. And remember, it is always better to under-correct rather than over-correct.

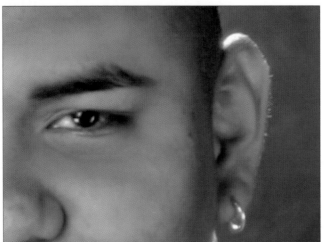

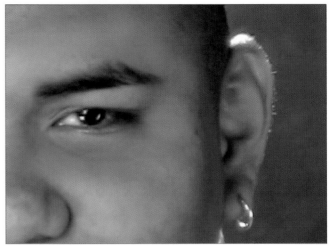

If you have to deal with correcting the ears after the shoot (above left), the Liquify filter will help (left). With some subtle work, a better look is achieved (above right).

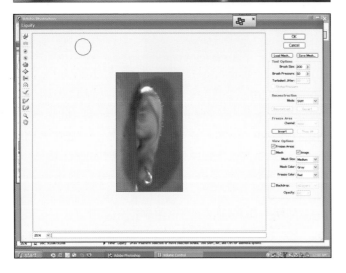

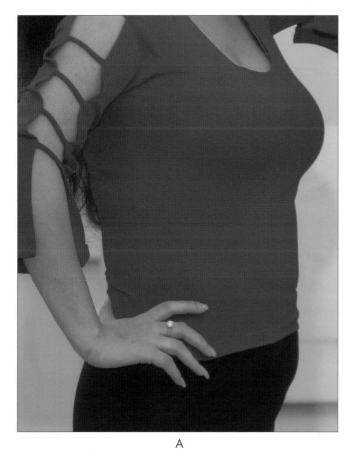

A

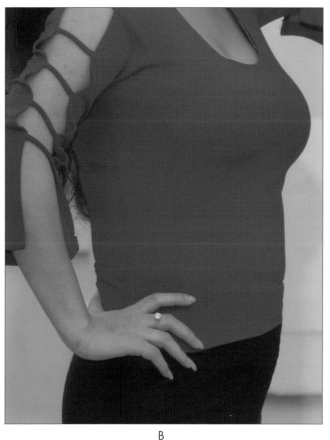

B

Even a thin person can have a less-than-flat stomach. To correct this, use the Liquify filter. Select the area of the bulge, liquify it, and then use a brush to nudge it so that it disappears.

■ THE NOSE

As noted on pages 41–42, the nose is defined by the shadows on the sides of it and the highlight that runs down the center. To reduce the apparent size of the nose, reduce the shadows. The best time to do this is by posing and lighting the client carefully when taking the image. If you need to retouch the image after the fact, use the Clone Stamp tool, set to a low opacity, and clone lighter skin from the cheek onto each side of the nose. As the shadows diminish, so will the apparent depth of the nose—but don't overdo it! You can also make the nose less noticeable by reducing the brightness of the highlight that runs the length of it, as well as the highlight that usually appears at the end of the nose.

■ THE EARS

The ears are usually best handled while photographing the portrait (see pages 40–41). If you have to deal with

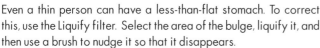

correcting the ears after the shoot, the Liquify filter will help. To begin, select the subject's entire head, then go to Filter>Liquify. A full-screen dialog box will appear with a preview of the selected area. Using a large brush, nudge the outer line of the ears inward toward the head, reducing their size.

■ TUMMY BULGE

The Liquify filter is also the best way to handle a less-than-flat-stomach when the subject is in a profile posi-

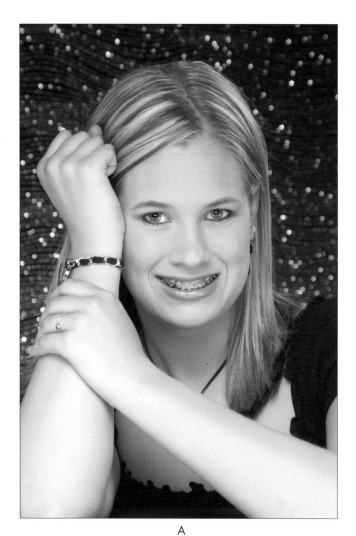

A

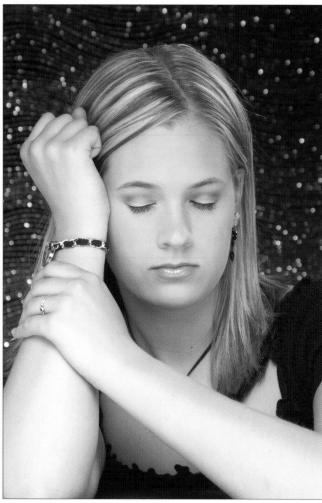

B

You have two poses, one with the eyes open and a large smile showing braces (A), the second with the eyes closed and a better expression on the mouth (B). Assuming the images are otherwise identical, you can place the image with the eyes closed on a layer over the image with the eyes open (C). Then, select the Eraser tool and erase the closed eyes from the top layer, revealing the open eyes (D). You have just made a customer happy in less than a minute!

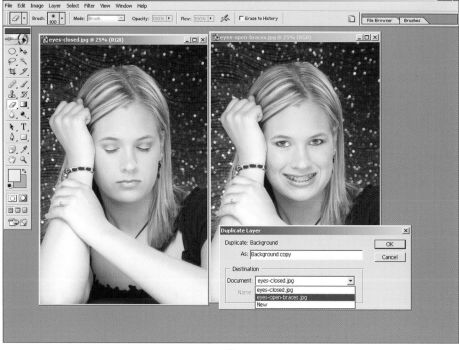

C

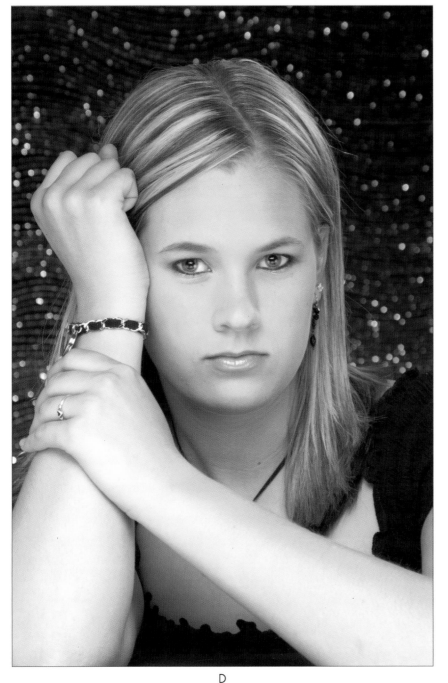

D

■ OPENING EYES

Opening eyes is something every photographer should learn how to do—it can often save a sale. We have never had to use this correction with our senior photography, because there is always another pose to select from, but we *have* had to use it in our prom and school-dance photography. We always take two shots of each couple at a dance, but there have been occasions where two, three, four or even five shots have been taken of a couple and either the girl or the guy (whoever is the blinker) has their eyes closed in all but one—and, of course, that's usually the one shot in which *their date* blinked! (On top of that, he or she will also turn out to be the son or daughter of the superintendent or principal of your largest school!) Of course we would swap heads for them—but wait! She likes her smile better in one of the poses where her eyes are closed, so she wants both of her eyes and his swapped.

To quickly switch the eyes in this kind of situation, we use the layer technique that was described on page 83. We start with the image with the girl's eyes open, then place the image with the correct smile on a layer over it. Select the Eraser tool and set the brush size slightly smaller than the size of the closed eyes on the good-smile layer. Erase the closed eyes, revealing the open eyes in the image underneath. Once it looks perfect, flatten the image (Layer>Flatten) and repeat the process with the image that has her date's eyes open. This works well, provided the images are composed exactly alike.

■ STRAY HAIRS

Another commonly requested correction is the removal of stray hairs. Even though we always look for this

tion. Select the stomach area (the tummy bulge) and, with the brush, push the line of the stomach back toward the body. Make sure that as the correction is done, lines don't get distorted. This is a very helpful tool for those clients whose outline could use some correction. I have used this on everything from wide waistlines to thick hips. Just make sure the line of the body part you are working on stays a line without unnatural hills and valleys (you will see what I mean when you use the tool!).

problem while photographing, some hair styles just naturally have hairs going in directions they shouldn't. The process of retouching a stray hair isn't difficult. I use the Clone Stamp tool, but this time with a high opacity and a hard-edged brush. This is because I want to completely cover the problem hairs with the background and do so without affecting any of the other hairs.

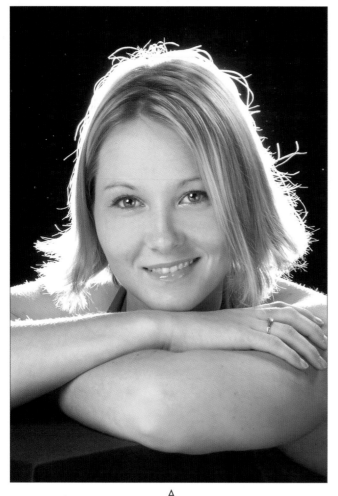

A

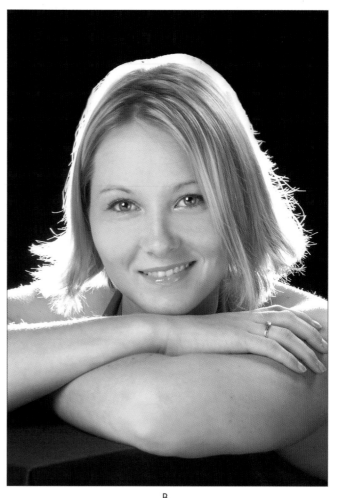

B

Stray hairs, especially when lit from behind, are a nasty correction to make (A). It's like taking a bite of bad food—the more you chew, the larger the problem seems to get. The correction technique is easy enough—use the Clone Stamp tool with a soft-edged brush and a opacity of about 75 percent to clone the background over each strand of hair (C)—the problem is knowing when to stop. You must follow each hair back to a point where it intersects with another hair (B). If you take out every stray hair, this too looks unnatural.

C

There are two problems that photographers often run into with this type of correction. First of all, they don't remove the stray hair or strand at a point where it looks natural. To avoid creating a chopped-off look, you must follow each stray hair back to a point where another hair or hair strand crosses it. This leads to the second problem, which is quoting enough time for the correction to be done properly. We can give most quotes without even examining the image. With hair, however, what may look like a five-minute job often takes twenty minutes or more. This is especially true when the hair is highlighted from behind and the strands are glowing.

■ BRACES

The last correction is one that I attempt to discourage clients from doing: removing braces. Removing braces is most often a no-win situation. It is expensive, because it is a complex correction, and it alters the look of a client. The easiest way to explain my feelings toward removing braces is found in every orthodontist's office on the day a patient's braces are to be removed. The patient has two reference points for how they should look when the see themselves in the mirror: with braces on or with the crooked teeth they started out with. Going in with my sons, I have heard comments from many young people seeing themselves for the first time in long while without braces—and most of the time, they're not positive. The person in the mirror isn't a person they recognize.

The same is true for this kind of correction. If you remove the braces from a person's teeth, often the reaction isn't going to be favorable. With this in mind, and factoring in the cost of the correction, I advise concerned clients to either take their photographs later, select a non-smiling pose, live with the braces, or have their orthodontist remove the wires and the front holders on each front tooth.

The basic problem with brace removal is that teeth have both color *and* texture. Also, the tone and color of each tooth changes dramatically from the center of the tooth to the edge of the tooth. Lastly, the very front teeth appear the lightest in tone, but the farther back you can see teeth, the darker the teeth appear. This is great number of variables, so basically you have to

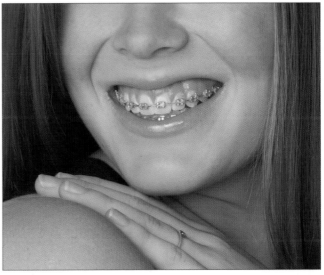

A

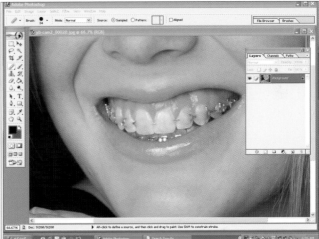

B

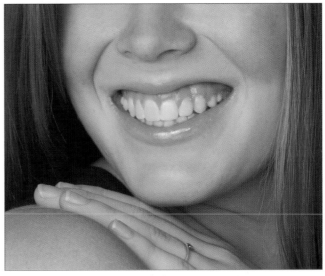

C

Removing braces (A) is a tricky task. It can be accomplished using the Clone tool (B) but getting good results can be very time consuming (and therefore, expensive).

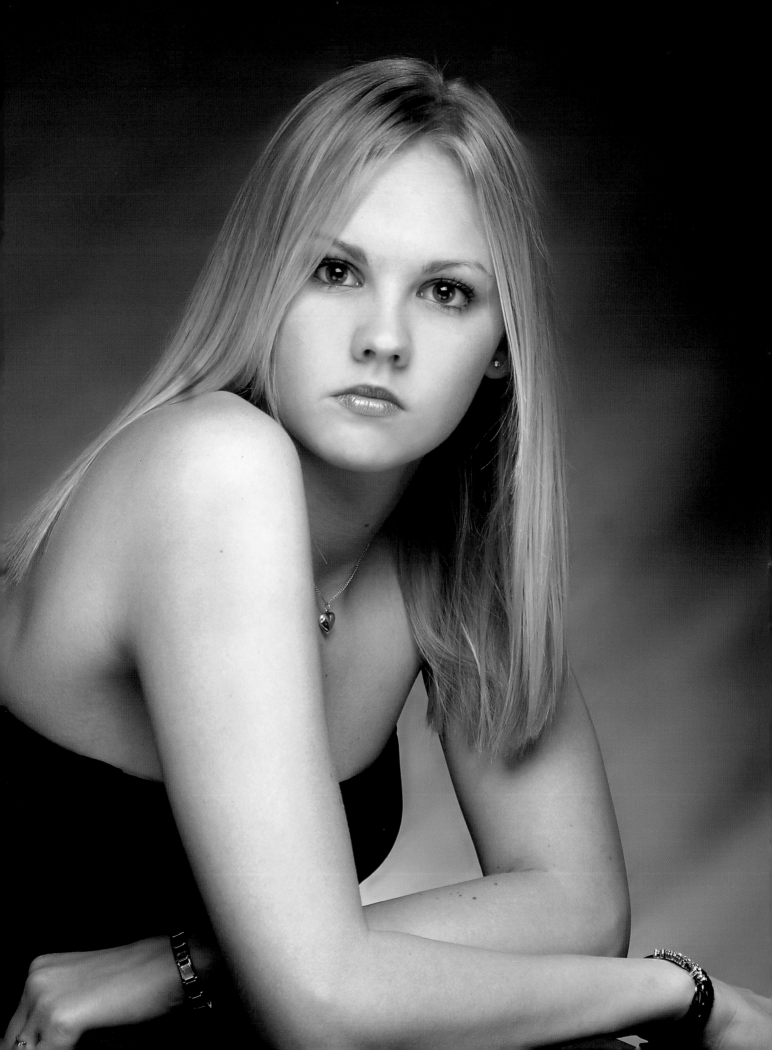

retouch each tooth individually and then make that tooth match the next.

You might ask yourself if it is necessary to take all these steps and spend all this time in the correction. My answer is yes. Brace removal is usually only requested in poses that have a larger head size (head-and-shoulders or waist-up poses). This usually means that the teeth have a great deal of detail, even in a 5x7-inch print size.

I have seen the corrections made by many retouchers, and they aren't pretty. The client's teeth look big, white, and without texture—and they're the first thing you see when you view the portrait. This breaks the most important rule for successful correction: the correction should never be noticeable.

With most corrections, we give a quote and do the enhancement before we print the final order. With more complex corrections, like braces, we print a sample of the correction that must be approved before we retouch all of the poses and print the order. This way, if the client doesn't like the braces removed, we only have to bill them for the retouching of one pose. It also assures me that the client is happy with the correction before we do the other poses.

■ **FINAL THOUGHTS**
This completes our look at the most commonly requested corrections that clients are usually willing to pay for. You will notice we didn't talk much about head-swapping or putting a third eye in the middle of a client's forehead, because the market for both procedures is fairly limited.

Although Photoshop has given the average photographer the ability to quickly retouch many problems that used to be to expensive to correct using film, it doesn't mean that the digital photographer must do his or her own corrections—or at least not *all* of them. It's just not cost effective to do so.

With most corrections, we give a quote and do the enhancement before we print the final order.

I know many photographers who provide the basic retouching for all their work and have their lab provide all major corrections, things that will be billed to the client. This is also a good approach for the photographer who lacks experience with Photoshop. You might do the simple corrections yourself and have your lab handle the more difficult enhancements until you gain the needed experience to do all of your own retouching (or build your business to the point where you can hire a staff member to do it).

When everything comes together (facing page), the result is a portrait that virtually sells itself.

CHAPTER TWELVE

THE PURSUIT OF PERFECTION

We live in a time where everything can (and if you are an American, *should*) be fixed by a pill, a plastic surgeon, or Photoshop—that's just the way it is! Once clients hear that you are digital photographer, they think you can fix anything! "I don't need to put on makeup," they think, "because the photographer will put it on for me!" What a wonderful, joyous time we live in!

Yes, I'm being a little bit sarcastic, but there is still a great deal of truth in this. People in general, and our clients specifically, *do* want to look perfect, but they *don't* want to get out of bed to shower and shave (so hitting the gym is pretty much out of the question). No one thinks anyone notices as they grow through the dress sizes and develop a neck like a linebacker. Then they have their portrait taken by you, you lucky dog. You strain through the session, using every trick in "the book" (actually, in *my* book!) to make this client happy with the way she appears. Then the moment of truth arrives—she looks at the proofs and shrieks, "Who *is* that wildebeest in my portraits? You claim to be a professional photographer and you create photographs that look like this? I've taken better photographs at home with my point-and-shoot!"

> Then the moment of truth arrives—she looks at the proofs and shrieks, "Who is that wildebeest in my portraits?"

So now what do you do? At this point, you have already explained about normal retouching, what it does and doesn't fix, as well as digital correction and the fact it is billed to the client, right? If you have, you can ask what it is the client doesn't like about the portraits. Once the client has calmed down, she will tell you the problem areas she worries about the most. It is your job to graciously explain the cause of these problems, then educate the client about what can be done to correct them.

■ WEIGHT ISSUES

Some of the most-requested corrections stem from clients being overweight. These problems can be imagined by the near-perfect female who feels her hips look too thick, or they may be very real concerns from a very overweight person who just wants to look better.

You will find the first signs of weight gain on a man at his waistline and the area under the chin. Women's extra weight also shows up in these areas, but the most common problem areas are the hips, thighs, and upper arms (if they are visible). Women also have issues with the appearance of rolls, which are often caused by their undergarments or the waistband of their pants.

Unlike typical corrections of the facial area, retouching the body requires more time and the use of multiple tools and techniques to fix a single problem. For example, if a woman with weight issues wants the rolls caused by her bra and waistband taken out and she wore a blouse with a strong pattern, that's going to be a difficult task. Not only must you remove the shadow area (where the clothing folds in) to smooth the appearance of the roll, but you must also keep the pattern of the clothing from becoming distorted.

A common weight-related correction is to make a double chin less noticeable. You'll recall we covered techniques for minimizing this concern with lighting and posing (see pages 39–40). If you need to address this issue at the retouching stage, the first step is to soften the line that separates the "natural" chin from the

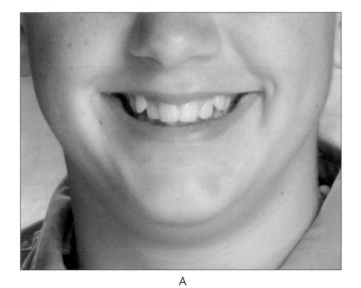

A

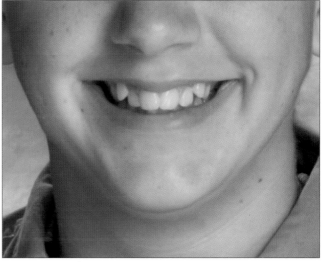

B

Both men and women have problems in the under-chin area (A). Using the Liquify filter, the lower part of the face (the chin and jowl area) can be reshaped (B). After some additional blending with the Clone tool, the result is natural looking and more flattering (C).

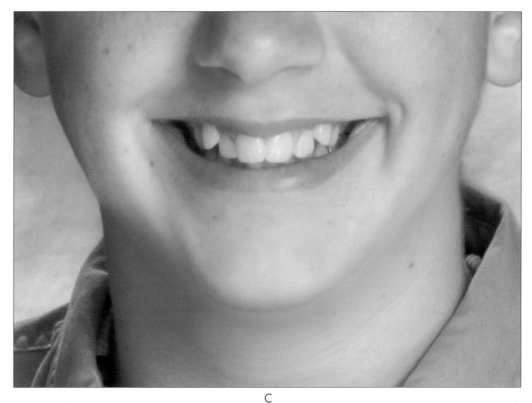

C

"double" chin. Without this fold, the double chin is less noticeable. The next step will depend on the shape of the double chin. If the double-chin area is small, you can often quickly fix the little bit of saggy skin by using the Liquify filter and selecting a tool to push the skin up. The success of this will depend on the area around the saggy skin. If it is just more skin, chances are no one will notice the distortion; if, on the other hand, the client has on a high-collared shirt or blouse, this procedure may not be possible.

If this is the case, you will need to clone over the saggy skin while maintaining a natural look. This typically requires smoothing out the hills and valleys. If you think of retouching this way, it makes it easier to know what needs to be cloned. Weight problems, as well as age, create hills and valleys in the skin/body. Hills are usually only noticed because of the valley or the shadow created in the valley. If you soften or eliminate the shadow in the valley, often you never notice the hill. You will find that not all double chins are fixable—at

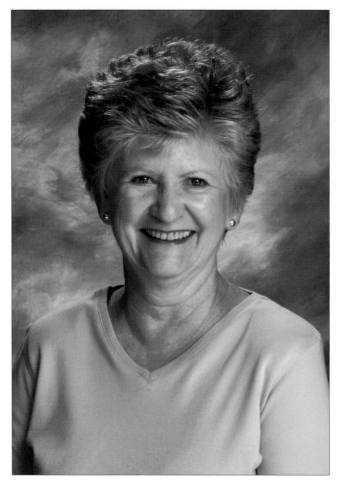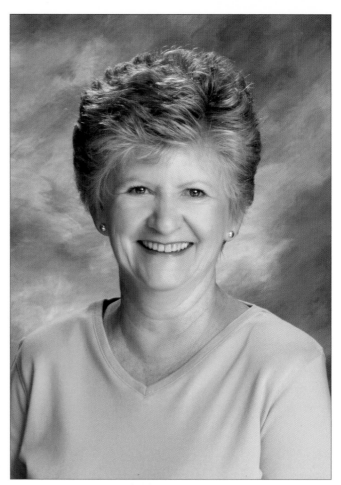

The retouching for a person over forty needs to address the signs of aging that occur in all of us (left). If we just eliminate wrinkles, it looks unnatural. Look at each area that is affected with age. The skin needs to have the lines softened, not eliminated. The eyes typically need to have he whites retouched and the catchlights enhanced. Our faces tend to widen as we age, and this needs to be addressed. We automatically whiten the teeth and soften the neck area. Only when you address all these areas do you come up with a complete correction that looks natural (right).

least not in an amount of time that can reasonably be billed to a client.

■ AGE-RELATED CONCERNS

In older clients, extra skin under the chin is related to the widening of the face on either side of the chin that occurs as we age. To remove the double chin without thinning the face in the jowl area would make the client look unnatural.

Wrinkles are part of a mature person, so they need to be softened, not eliminated. Often, the subject's eyes will need enhancement to whiten the whites and bring back the sparkle the eyes once had. The skin on the neck also needs to be smoothed, softening the cords that often become visible with age. When dealing with mature clients, we also brighten and whiten their teeth (unless they have dentures, which obviously don't age).

In a portrait of a mature person, *all* of these areas needed to be addressed in order for the correction to make sense visually. This would be considered standard retouching when working with mature clients.

■ MULTIPLE ISSUES

As noted above, you must often deal with multiple issues in order to have the corrected portrait look natural. For example, if the client has a weight issue, how can you correct some of the problem areas without addressing all of them? Let's say you have a heavy girl in a sleeveless top and she asks that you make her arms smaller. If you just make her arms smaller without addressing her larger hips and waistline, it will just refocus her attention from one of her problem areas to another. Therefore, when you give her the estimate, you should quote enough time to address all of the weight issues instead of just the one that bothers her the most.

A problem with correcting weight issues is that a particular correction will work with a client in one pose and not in another. You can stretch a person as discussed on page 93, but this only works if the client is in a standing pose. You can work with the Liquify filter—but only if the part of the body you need to correct has a background without distinct lines or patterns directly behind the area you need to correct.

Look through the photos in this book to see how we corrected the weight issues for these clients. Not every tool work will work with every pose, so you just have to get imaginative and figure out the fastest way to make any given correction.

■ EXTREME CORRECTIONS

Some corrective techniques fall into a category I call "what photographers do when they have too much time on their hands or want to fill seat at a Photoshop

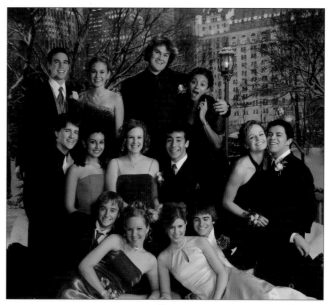
A

B

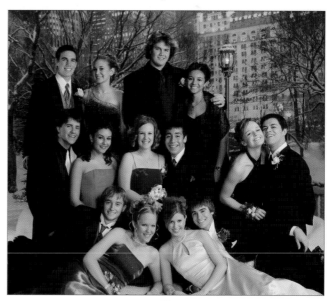
C

When you have two or more images of the same group, head swapping can be used to fix blinking or improve the overall facial expressions. Images A and B are portraits of the same group. By combining some of the expressions from one with the other you can get the best of both. Here, I began with A because it had more good facial expressions. The two heads I swapped out were in the center row—the young man on the left and the blond girl near the center with her tongue sticking out. They were replaced with the faces from B.

I began with the Extract tool (Filter>Extract), selecting the Highlighter tool and outlining the young man's head in image B that I wanted to move onto image A (I zoomed in to make the selection accurate). Once the head was outlined, I chose the fill tool and clicked within the outline to select the entire face. I hit OK, then clicked and dragged the extracted head into image A. After positioning it over the old head, some of the original head was still visible. To remove this, I used the Clone tool to cover the area with fabric from the coat of the fellow behind our subject.

To replace the young lady's head, I followed the same basic procedure. A little extra background was accidentally extracted with the head, so the Eraser tool was used (with a soft brush) to remove this after the head was in position on an overlying layer in image A. The extracted areas that covered her necklace were also erased.

With both heads, the final step was to use the Clone tool to clean up the intersection line between the new heads and the old photo. The result was a new photo with only the best smiles (C)!

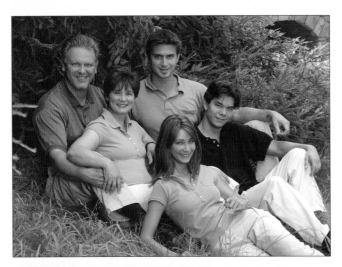

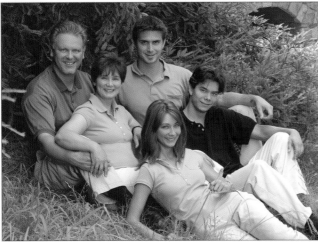

To change the color of a subject's outfit, isolate the item you want to change by selecting it using any of Photoshop's selection tools (the Magic Wand, Lasso, etc.). Next, go to Image>Adjustments> Hue/Saturation. Select the appropriate color from the Edit pull-down menu (in this case, for example, cyan was chosen, since that's the color in the young woman's shirt that needed to change). Finally, adjust the sliders to change the color as you like.

seminar." They are used when making more extreme corrections—the kind that most clients could really never afford to pay for but that photographers like to know how to do anyway!

■ GUIDING YOUR CLIENTS

Clients need to be guided through their decisions when it comes to retouching. How much is really needed? Is a correction really worth the cost of doing it, or is the client better off selecting another pose, or even just living with the pose without the correction?

Everyone needs to understand that there is a difference between "great" and "perfect." Almost every meal I have is edible; it is seldom perfect. Although I eat out often and have been fortunate enough to eat at some truly exceptional restaurants, I have only had one *perfect* meal. We showed up early and were seated at great table right away. We had the best waiter we have ever had, the food was perfect, and my wife wore a beautiful dress (which completed the experience). Although that was the only perfect meal I have had, I have enjoyed many *great* meals. I've been happy with my experience and recommended those restaurants to others.

Many photographers get very stressed trying to achieve *perfection* when they have already achieved *greatness*. No matter how beautiful the image, they always say, "Well, I wish I had done this or that differently." They won the print competition, but it wasn't good enough. When you create a beautiful image for your client and know that perfection can be achieved without an incredible expense, then suggest it. If great is as good as it can get, be honest; tell the client that the image is beautiful and it doesn't need correction.

Clients also need to be advised about all the options that Photoshop has given us. With film, I shot low-key images with a black vignette and high-key images with a clear crinkle vignette—unless of course I didn't want to use a vignette. The choice was mine and the client accepted what I created. With digital, we don't shoot with any vignettes, because they are so easy to add in Photoshop. The client can put any type of vignette on any image—and that's a choice that most clients can't make without some help. You have to explain their options and make suggestion as to what they should do.

I am a firm believer in the client calling the shots and being given as many options as possible. We have always allowed clients to select the backgrounds and poses they want done in their session. With girls, the mothers typically help with the selection. For years, I wondered what was wrong with our clients—the mother would pick out a full-length pose from the sample books, we would photograph it exactly like the sample portrait, and yet when the mother looked at it she didn't like it because it was "too far away."

I began to understand the situation better one day when I was up in the front of the studio and was asked to talk with a assertive mother suffering from this problem. The mother told me her daughter was too far away and she couldn't see her face. I explained that her daughter was photographed in the same way as the sample portrait she selected. The mother insisted the sample portrait was closer. I pulled it out of the book to compare the two photographs and they were identical. Yet, even with both prints in front of her she said her daughter looked smaller.

As I was talking with her, I realized something that I never thought of before. When a mother looks a *someone else's* child, she sees the beauty in the pose, the set, and the lighting; when a mother looks at *her own* child, she wants to see her child. At this point, I realized that while clients need to make their own decisions, they also need guidance to make the right choices. We now make it a point to photograph each full-length idea in a close-up as well.

As we expand what is possible with digital and the number of options we offer our clients grows, so does the amount of guidance our clients need to make the decision that is best for them. No matter how detailed your advice to clients, however, you should also be sure to put everything in writing. If you are doing digital corrections, put in writing what the client can expect from it, state what the cost is, and then have them sign it. This eliminates any potential conflict between you and your clients.

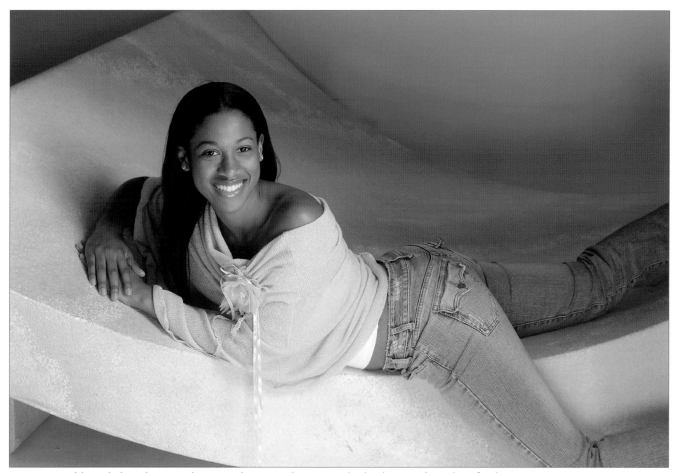

More is possible with digital, so our clients need more guidance to make the decision that is best for them.

CHAPTER THIRTEEN

WORKING QUICKLY IN PHOTOSHOP

Time is money. Whether you are paying staff to work on your images or giving up your own free time or billable hours, every minute you are on the computer is a minute that costs you profit. With that in mind, I have some suggestions for getting the most out of your time and money.

■ REMOVE THE GAMES

The first suggestion is especially important if you have your staff work on your images. Remove all games from each computer in your studio and never have Internet access on the stations where you will be working on your images. I can't count the number of times I have walked in on staff member playing solitaire. Games

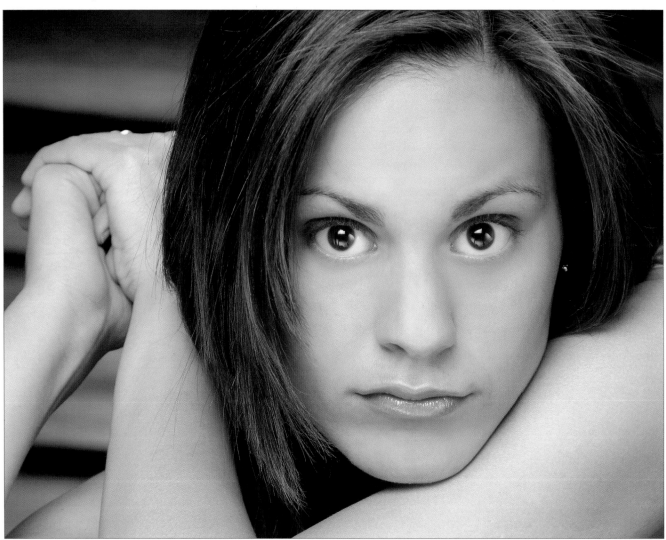

Achieving top quality results and efficiency in imaging requires undisturbed concentration.

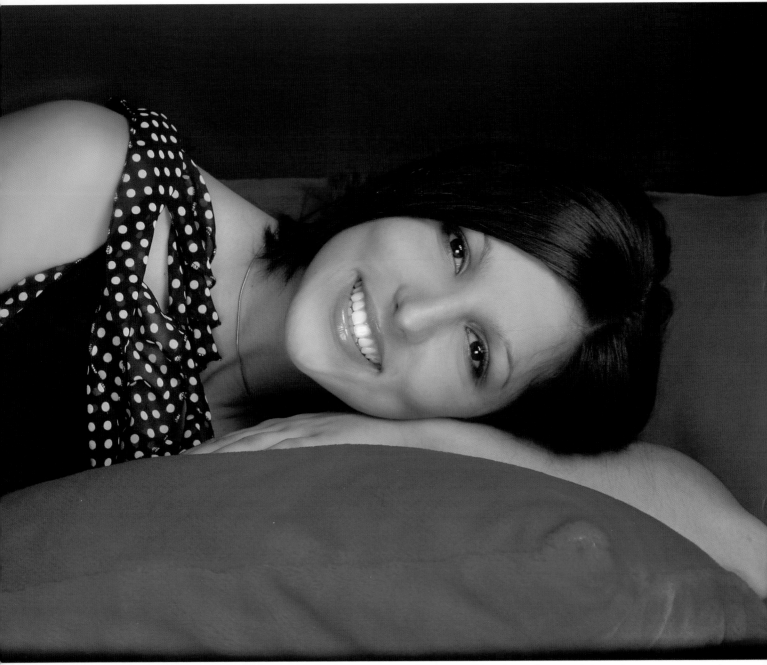

An important timesaver is learning Photoshop's keyboard shortcuts—combinations of keys that will accomplish any function or command.

should be outlawed in computers produced for business use. The Internet not only wastes time, but no matter how good your virus scan is you risk down time and lost work.

■ ISOLATION

Isolation is another important factor in profiting from digital correction. Most people can't work together without talking. Working on digital files requires concentration. Employees needs to have breaks and time away from digital production, but make it as difficult as possible for your employees to talk freely. Use large partitions or black curtains around each desk—whatever it takes to keep each person at their station and focused on the job at hand.

In the studio, we believe in training our employees well. I show each person how much time is wasted when you stop what you are doing to talk with a coworker. The biggest problem is that, unlike talking on the phone to a spouse or boyfriend, when one employee is talking to another I have *two* people on the clock doing nothing!

To that end, we often look for quiet people to fill our production positions. The worst person to put into a production situation is a salesperson. At one point, I thought (frugal person that I am) we could fill in the time of some our salespeople by having them help with the retouching on the orders they had taken. Most of them were already familiar with Photoshop and quickly understood the process. The one problem I didn't foresee was that, because we hire salespeople who are friendly and love people, they *talk* and *talk* and *talk*. We actually got less work out of five people than we did the original three! Each time I went into the lab, the gossip session abruptly ended and everyone scrambled back to their computers.

■ KEYBOARD SHORTCUTS

Another important timesaver is learning Photoshop's many keyboard shortcuts—combinations of keys that will accomplish any function or command. This saves a huge amount of time for the people involved in your production work.

■ ACTIONS AND BATCH PROCESSING

Actions and batch processing are probably the greatest labor-saving devices available to photographers doing digital correction. An action is a recorded digital process containing everything you want done to achieve a particular type of adjustment. Once you've recorded the steps for one image, you can use the action to replay them at will, applying the identical steps to any other image needing the same adjustments.

To create an action, open an image. Then, open the actions palette (Window> Actions). Click on the drop-down menu at

Actions and batch processing are probably the greatest labor-saving devices available to photographers doing digital correction.

the upper-right corner of the palette and select New Action. Name the action as you like, then hit Record. Every change you make to the image will be recorded until you hit the Stop button (located at the bottom of the actions palette).

Actions not only increase the speed at which you accomplish your work but also ensure consistency. For example, we use an action to convert our color images to black & white. This action is installed in each sales

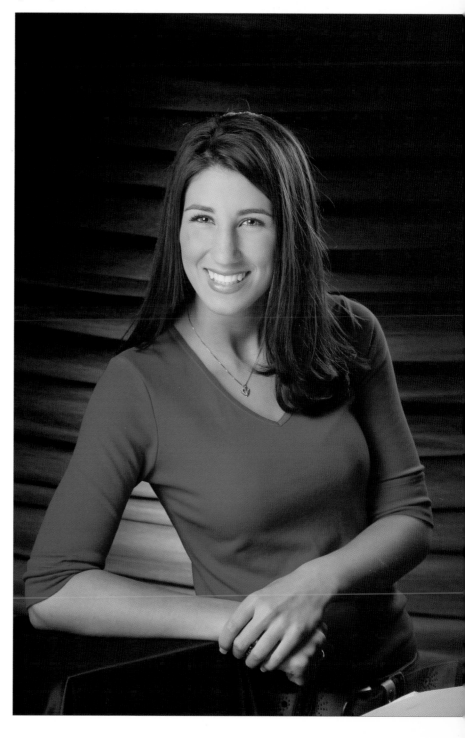

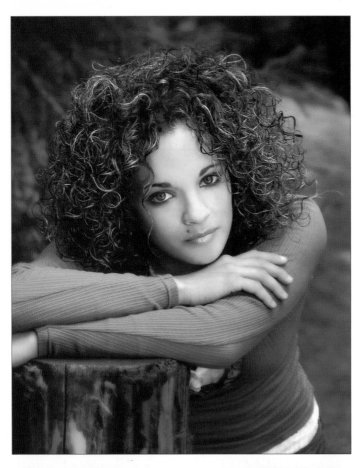

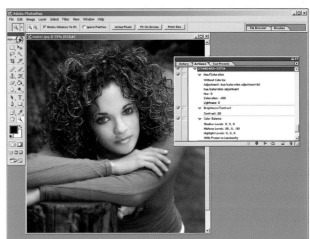

When creating sepia-toned images, using an action ensures that the color will look just the way the client expects—and will match perfectly from image to image.

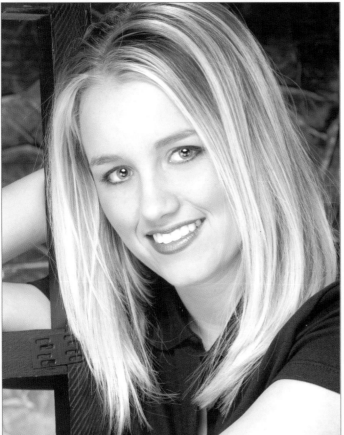

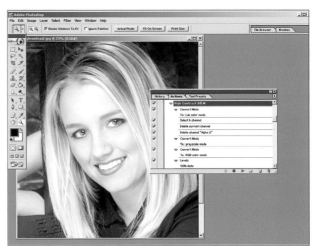

The creation of high-contrast black & white portraits can also be automated with an action.

computer. When viewing images with a client, all the salesperson has to do is hit the play button and the color image is quickly converted. Consistency is achieved, because the same action is used in all the computers in the lab—so what the client sees is exactly what they get.

A batch process (File>Automate>Batch) lets you apply any given action to an entire folder of files. Batch processing works well when you have a large number of files that all need similar corrections. This can save you a lot of time.

Let me give you an example. To prepare our images for printing, we open all the images that a client has ordered from and retouch each pose. Then we start recording a new action, as described above. The first thing we do is select Levels and make any needed adjustments, then we add saturation, sharpen the image slightly, and save the image into a file we create called "Current Order." Once we save the image, we crop it to 4x5 inches and then re-save the cropped image into a subfolder called "Proofs." Then we select Edit>Step Backward, which takes us back to the uncropped image. Now, we crop the image to 8x10 inches and save the image into a second subfolder titled "8x10." We then select Edit>Step Backward again, then crop the original image to 5x7 inches and save into a third subfolder called "5x7." We then select Edit>Step Backward a final time, taking us back to the original image. We then stop the recording of the action.

At this point, we have created an action that can be used to color correct each image from the session and provide a 4x5-inch file for the folio, a 5x7-inch file for either 5x7-inch prints or wallets, and an 8x10-inch file to package the 8x10- and 4x5-inch prints. It then leaves

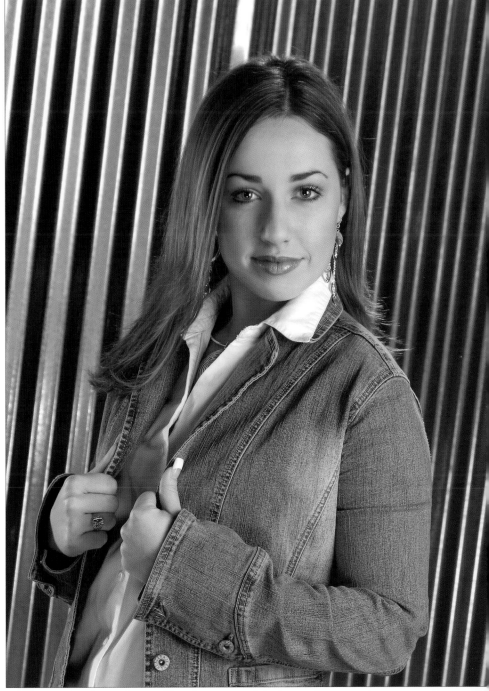

Actions can even be used to quickly color correct all the images from a session.

the original image open for any larger prints needed from this file. It can be reused for each and every order placed from the session.

While this sounds good, many photographers are thinking, "Wait a minute! I like to adjust my color for each pose specifically, not have a general correction. And what about cropping? Not every image is going to be cropped the same!" That's why actions have a stop feature. On the left side of each command in the

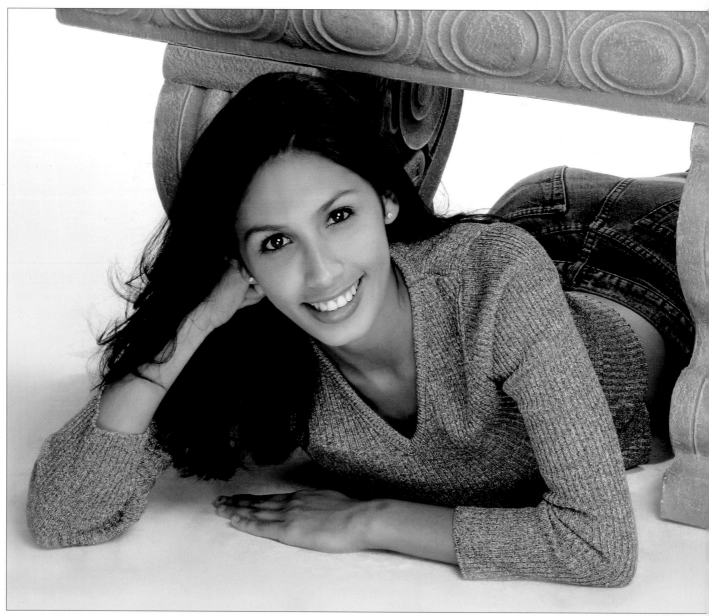

Actions will save time and money, so sit down and think of ways to automate your work with actions.

actions palette is a box you can highlight to make the action.

We also have an action made to place eight opened 4x5-inch files place onto a 10x16-inch sheet, flatten it, turn it in the correct direction to go through the printer, then save it in the "Print" sub-file of the "Current Order" file (where everything goes before it goes to the printer).

Most of our special-effects portraits are also created using actions. When we use layers to create an effect, we have an action prepare the layers, add textures or effects, stop so we can erase the area we want to show through, then restart and flatten the completed image.

Using actions requires some forethought. Many photographer create a specific action that is used for only one order, then the delete that action only to create another identical action for the next order, because they want the action to save the image into a specific client's folder rather than a generic folder. This wastes time. We use generic folders for our actions, then transfer the images to a client folder or burn the work to CD so we don't waste time constantly creating actions.

Actions will save time and money, so sit down and think of ways to automate your work with actions—and remember to keep actions generic so they will work with all your images.

What photography student couldn't take a beautiful portrait of a beautiful person? Reality is exactly what the camera is designed to record. Unfortunately, many photographers base their estimation of their own level of expertise on their best photographs of their most beautiful clients. The problem is, these aren't the images that will sustain your business and your livelihood. To be a successful professional and enjoy a profit from every session (not just the sessions of beautiful people), you need to evaluate your least photogenic clients and see how you made them look.

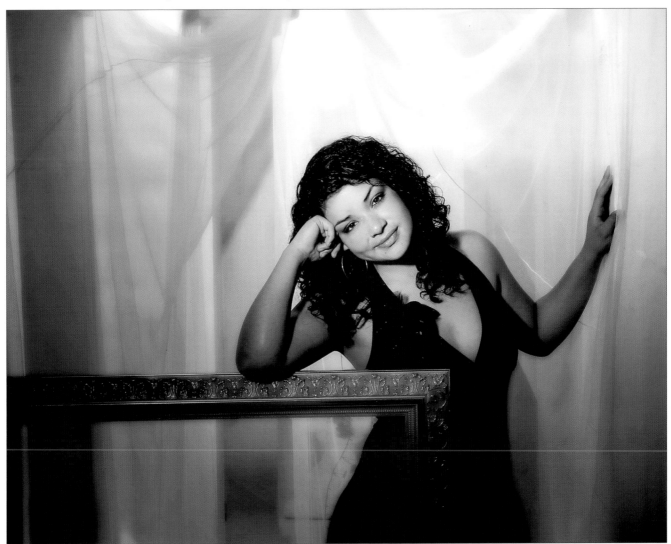

Digital technology has given today's professional photographer many new options and opportunities for producing beautiful images—but it's also become an expensive crutch for those who don't want to master their craft.

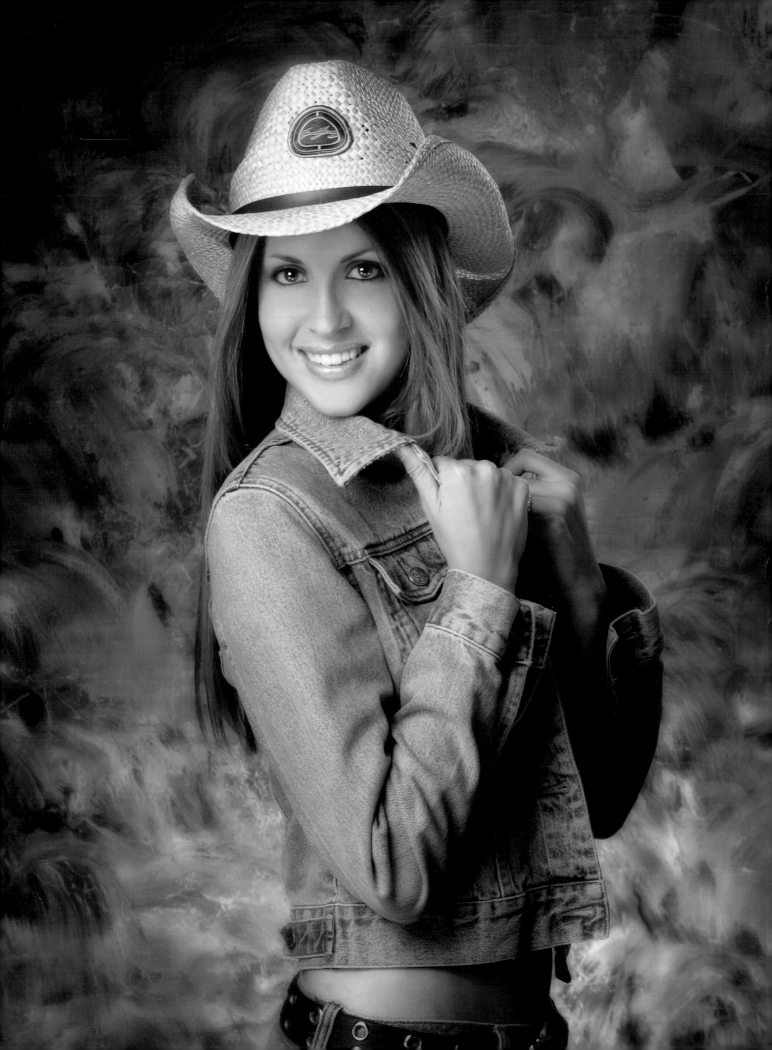

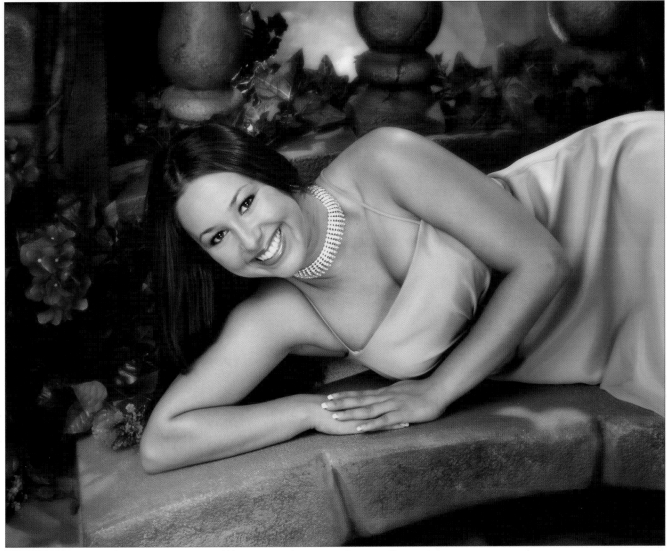

If I could leave you with one message, it would be to care about your clients—all your clients.

Do you give them a version of reality that they can live with, or is your mind working desperately to save your ego, by telling yourself, "What do you expect, she or he was too overweight, too short, too homely, etc.?"

When I was a young professional and trying to define the direction of my business, I really tried to make each client look his or her best. Quite frankly, in those days I couldn't afford to lose any clients. On one occasion, I had photographed a young senior girl who was probably 60 to 80 pounds overweight. I used a very contrasty light to have a very dark shadow, thinning the face. I used poses that hid her very large double chin from the perspective of the camera. I picked out her clothing, all of which was very dark, and used her long hair to soften the size of her shoulders and arms. At that point in time in the studio, I was both the

photographer *and* the person who delivered the proofs to the client. When this girl and her mother came in to the studio and started to look at her proofs, the mother started to cry. The mother said, "I have always told my daughter that, despite her weight, she is a beautiful young lady and these portraits show the beautiful young lady she is." The mother gave me a hug and thanked me. This is a session I will never forget, because for the first time I understood how much a professional portrait means to our clients.

Digital technology has given today's professional photographer many new options and opportunities for achieving this goal—but it's also become an expensive crutch for those who don't want to master their craft. Photoshop has provided us with a way to improve the basic retouching that all finished portraits should have,

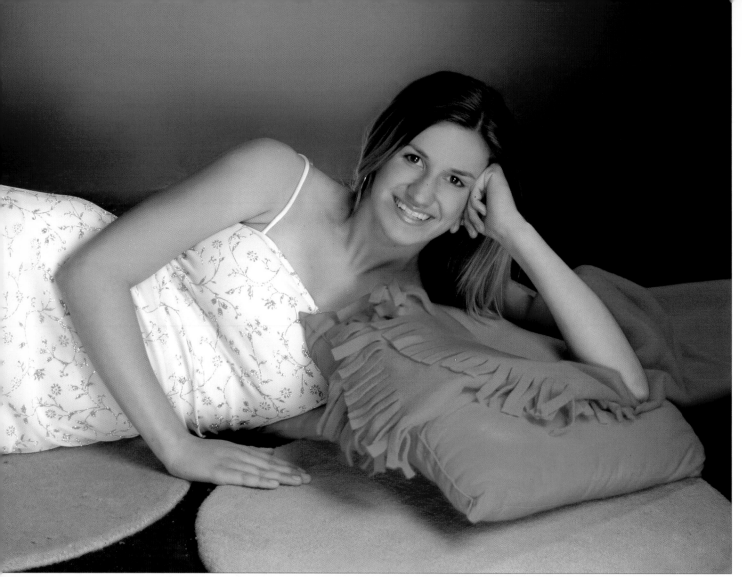

Measure your growth on how good you can make each client look, not on your best photographs of your most beautiful clients.

as well as cleaning up white floors, marks on sets, and other imperfections that occur in a busy studio—things your clients shouldn't have to suffer with. I am a firm believer in offering a client the very best product that is possible, but if you find that you are taking your great images and making them perfect without an increase in prices, you are on a slippery slope.

So, if I could leave you with one message, it would be to care about your clients—all your clients. Put the same effort into a session with a person who has obvious flaws as you do into a session with the perfect people you invite to come in for test sessions. Measure your growth on how good you can make each client look, not on your best photographs of your most beautiful clients. Use digital to help you achieve this goal, but do so wisely, making sure you'll still be in business the next time your very satisfied clients are in need of your services.

ABOUT THE AUTHOR

Jeff Smith is a professional photographer and the owner of two very successful studios in central California. His numerous articles have appeared in *Rangefinder, Professional Photographer,* and *Studio Photography and Design* magazines. Jeff has been a featured speaker at the Senior Photographers International Convention, as well as at numerous seminars for professional photographers. He has written numerous books, including *Outdoor and Location Portrait Photography, Posing for Portrait Photography, Professional Digital Portrait Photography,* and *Success in Portrait Photography* (all from Amherst Media®). His common-sense approach to photography and business makes the information he presents both practical and very easy to understand.

INDEX

Other books by Jeff Smith . . .

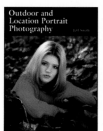

OUTDOOR AND LOCATION PORTRAIT PHOTOGRAPHY, 2nd Ed.
Learn to work with natural light, select locations, and make clients look their best. Packed with step-by-step discussions and illustrations to help you shoot like a pro! $34.95 list, 8½x11, 128p, 80 color photos, index, order no. 1632.

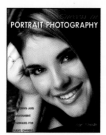

SUCCESS IN PORTRAIT PHOTOGRAPHY
Many photographers realize too late that camera skills alone do not ensure success. This book will teach photographers how to run savvy marketing campaigns, attract clients, and provide top-notch customer service. $29.95 list, 8½x11, 128p, 100 color photos, order no. 1748.

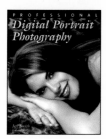

PROFESSIONAL DIGITAL PORTRAIT PHOTOGRAPHY
Because the learning curve is so steep, making the transition to digital can be frustrating. Author Jeff Smith shows readers how to shoot, edit, and retouch their images—while avoiding common pitfalls. $29.95 list, 8½x11, 128p, 100 color photos, order no. 1750.

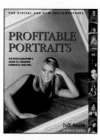

PROFITABLE PORTRAITS
THE PHOTOGRAPHER'S GUIDE TO CREATING PORTRAITS THAT SELL
Learn how to design images that are precisely tailored to your clients' tastes—portraits that will practically sell themselves! $29.95 list, 8½x11, 128p, 100 color photos, index, order no. 1797.

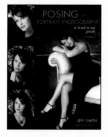

POSING FOR PORTRAIT PHOTOGRAPHY
A HEAD-TO-TOE GUIDE
Author Jeff Smith teaches surefire techniques for fine-tuning every aspect of the pose for the most flattering results. $34.95 list, 8½x11, 128p, 150 color photos, index, order no. 1786.

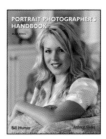

PORTRAIT PHOTOGRAPHER'S HANDBOOK, 2nd Ed.
Bill Hurter
Bill Hurter has compiled a step-by-step guide to portraiture that easily leads the reader through all phases of portrait photography. This book will be an asset to experienced photographers and beginners alike. $29.95 list, 8½x11, 128p, 175 color photos, order no. 1708.

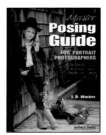

MASTER POSING GUIDE FOR PORTRAIT PHOTOGRAPHERS
J. D. Wacker
Learn the techniques you need to pose single portrait subjects, couples, and groups for studio or location portraits. Includes techniques for photographing weddings, teams, children, special events, and much more. $34.95 list, 8½x11, 128p, 80 photos, order no. 1722.

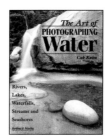

THE ART OF PHOTOGRAPHING WATER
Cub Kahn
Learn to capture the dazzling interplay of light and water with this beautiful, compelling, and comprehensive book. Packed with practical information you can use right away to improve your images! $29.95 list, 8½x11, 128p, 70 color photos, order no. 1724.

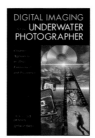

DIGITAL IMAGING FOR THE UNDERWATER PHOTOGRAPHER, 2nd Ed.
Jack and Sue Drafahl
This book will teach readers how to improve their underwater images with digital image-enhancement techniques. This book covers all the bases—from color balancing your monitor, to scanning, to output and storage. $39.95 list, 6x9, 224p, 240 color photos, order no. 1727.

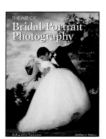

THE ART OF BRIDAL PORTRAIT PHOTOGRAPHY
Marty Seefer
Learn to give every client your best and create timeless images that are sure to become family heirlooms. Seefer takes readers through every step of the bridal shoot, ensuring flawless results. $29.95 list, 8½x11, 128p, 70 color photos, order no. 1730.

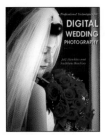

PROFESSIONAL TECHNIQUES FOR
DIGITAL WEDDING PHOTOGRAPHY, 2nd Ed.

Jeff Hawkins and Kathleen Hawkins

From selecting equipment, to marketing, to building a digital workflow, this book teaches how to make digital work for you. $34.95 list, 8½x11, 128p, 85 color images, order no. 1735.

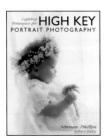

LIGHTING TECHNIQUES FOR
HIGH KEY PORTRAIT PHOTOGRAPHY

Norman Phillips

Learn to meet the challenges of high key portrait photography and produce images your clients will adore. $29.95 list, 8½x11, 128p, 100 color photos, order no. 1736.

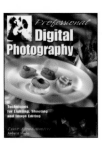

PROFESSIONAL DIGITAL PHOTOGRAPHY

Dave Montizambert

From monitor calibration, to color balancing, to creating advanced artistic effects, this book provides those skilled in basic digital imaging with the techniques they need to take their photography to the next level. $29.95 list, 8½x11, 128p, 120 color photos, order no. 1739.

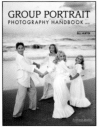

GROUP PORTRAIT PHOTOGRAPHY HANDBOOK, 2nd Ed.

Bill Hurter

Featuring over 100 images by top photographers, this book offers practical techniques for composing, lighting, and posing group portraits—whether in the studio or on location. $34.95 list, 8½x11, 128p, 120 color photos, order no. 1740.

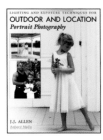

LIGHTING AND EXPOSURE TECHNIQUES FOR
OUTDOOR AND LOCATION PORTRAIT PHOTOGRAPHY

J. J. Allen

Meet the challenges of changing light and complex settings with techniques that help you achieve great images every time. $34.95 list, 8½x11, 128p, 150 color photos, order no. 1741.

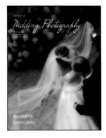

THE BEST OF WEDDING PHOTOGRAPHY, 2nd Ed.

Bill Hurter

Learn how the top wedding photographers in the industry transform special moments into lasting romantic treasures with the posing, lighting, album design, and customer service pointers found in this book. $34.95 list, 8½x11, 128p, 150 color photos, order no. 1747.

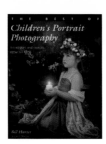

THE BEST OF CHILDREN'S PORTRAIT PHOTOGRAPHY

Bill Hurter

Rangefinder editor Bill Hurter draws upon the experience and work of top professional photographers, uncovering the creative and technical skills they use to create their magical portraits of these young subejcts. $29.95 list, 8½x11, 128p, 150 color photos, order no. 1752.

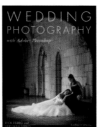

WEDDING PHOTOGRAPHY WITH ADOBE® PHOTOSHOP®

Rick Ferro and Deborah Lynn Ferro

Get the skills you need to make your images look their best, add artistic effects, and boost your wedding photography sales with savvy marketing ideas. $34.95 list, 8½x11, 128p, 100 color images, index, order no. 1753.

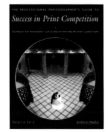

PROFESSIONAL PHOTOGRAPHER'S GUIDE TO
SUCCESS IN PRINT COMPETITION

Patrick Rice

Learn from PPA and WPPI judges how you can improve your print presentations and increase your scores. $29.95 list, 8½x11, 128p, 100 color photos, index, order no. 1754.

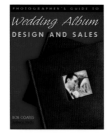

PHOTOGRAPHER'S GUIDE TO
WEDDING ALBUM DESIGN AND SALES

Bob Coates

Enhance your income and creativity with these techniques from top wedding photographers. $29.95 list, 8½x11, 128p, 150 color photos, index, order no. 1757.

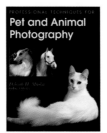

PROFESSIONAL TECHNIQUES FOR
PET AND ANIMAL PHOTOGRAPHY

Debrah H. Muska

Adapt your portrait skills to meet the challenges of pet photography, creating images for both owners and breeders. $29.95 list, 8½x11, 128p, 110 color photos, index, order no. 1759.

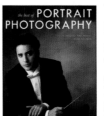

THE BEST OF PORTRAIT PHOTOGRAPHY

Bill Hurter

View outstanding images from top professionals and learn how they create their masterful images. Includes techniques for classic and contemporary portraits. $29.95 list, 8½x11, 128p, 200 color photos, index, order no. 1760.

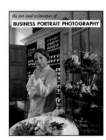

THE ART AND TECHNIQUES OF
BUSINESS PORTRAIT PHOTOGRAPHY
Andre Amyot

Learn the business and creative skills photographers need to compete successfully in this challenging field. $29.95 list, 8½x11, 128p, 100 color photos, index, order no. 1762.

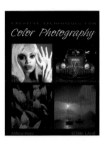

CREATIVE TECHNIQUES FOR COLOR PHOTOGRAPHY
Bobbi Lane

Learn how to render color precisely, whether you are shooting digitally or on film. Also includes creative techniques for cross processing, color infrared, and more. $29.95 list, 8½x11, 128p, 250 color photos, index, order no. 1764.

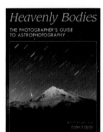

HEAVENLY BODIES
THE PHOTOGRAPHER'S GUIDE TO ASTROPHOTOGRAPHY
Bert P. Krages, Esq.

Learn to capture the beauty of the night sky with a 35mm camera. Tracking and telescope techniques are also covered. $29.95 list, 8½x11, 128p, 100 color photos, index, order no. 1769.

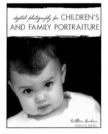

DIGITAL PHOTOGRAPHY FOR CHILDREN'S AND FAMILY PORTRAITURE
Kathleen Hawkins

Discover how digital photography can boost your sales, enhance your creativity, and improve your studio's workflow. $29.95 list, 8½x11, 128p, 130 color images, index, order no. 1770.

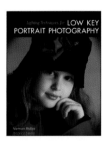

LIGHTING TECHNIQUES FOR
LOW KEY PORTRAIT PHOTOGRAPHY
Norman Phillips

Learn to create the dark tones and dramatic lighting that typify this classic portrait style. $29.95 list, 8½x11, 128p, 100 color photos, index, order no. 1773.

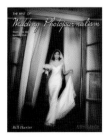

THE BEST OF WEDDING PHOTOJOURNALISM
Bill Hurter

Learn how top professionals capture these fleeting moments of laughter, tears, and romance. Features images from over twenty renowned wedding photographers. $34.95 list, 8½x11, 128p, 150 color photos, index, order no. 1774.

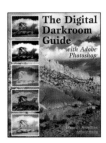

THE DIGITAL DARKROOM GUIDE WITH ADOBE® PHOTOSHOP®
Maurice Hamilton

Bring the skills and control of the photographic darkroom to your desktop with this complete manual. $29.95 list, 8½x11, 128p, 140 color images, index, order no. 1775.

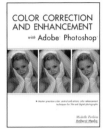

COLOR CORRECTION AND ENHANCEMENT WITH ADOBE® PHOTOSHOP®
Michelle Perkins

Master precision color correction and artistic color enhancement techniques for scanned and digital photos. $29.95 list, 8½x11, 128p, 300 color images, index, order no. 1776.

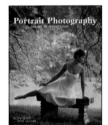

PORTRAIT PHOTOGRAPHY
THE ART OF SEEING LIGHT
Don Blair with Peter Skinner

Learn to harness the best light both in studio and on location, and get the secrets behind the magical portraiture captured by this legendary photographer. $29.95 list, 8½x11, 128p, 100 color photos, index, order no. 1783.

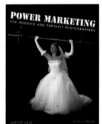

POWER MARKETING FOR WEDDING AND PORTRAIT PHOTOGRAPHERS
Mitche Graf

Set your business apart and create clients for life with this comprehensive guide to achieving your professional goals. $29.95 list, 8½x11, 128p, 100 color images, index, order no. 1788.

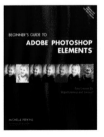

BEGINNER'S GUIDE TO ADOBE® PHOTOSHOP® ELEMENTS®
Michelle Perkins

Packed with easy lessons for improving virtually every aspect of your images—from color balance, to creative effects, and more. $29.95 list, 8½x11, 128p, 300 color images, index, order no. 1790.

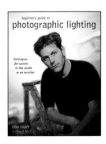

BEGINNER'S GUIDE TO PHOTOGRAPHIC LIGHTING
Don Marr

Create high-impact photographs of any subject with Marr's simple techniques. From edgy and dynamic to subdued and natural, this book will show you how to get the myriad effects you're after. $29.95 list, 8½x11, 128p, 150 color photos, index, order no. 1785.

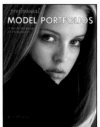

PROFESSIONAL
MODEL PORTFOLIOS

A STEP-BY-STEP GUIDE FOR PHOTOGRAPHERS

Billy Pegram

Learn how to create dazzling portfolios that will get your clients noticed—and hired! $34.95 list, 8½x11, 128p, 100 color images, index, order no. 1789.

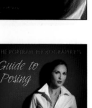

THE PORTRAIT PHOTOGRAPHER'S
GUIDE TO POSING

Bill Hurter

Posing can make or break an image. Now you can get the posing tips and techniques that have propelled the finest portrait photographers in the industry to the top. $34.95 list, 8½x11, 128p, 200 color photos, index, order no. 1779.

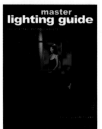

MASTER LIGHTING GUIDE

FOR PORTRAIT PHOTOGRAPHERS

Christopher Grey

Efficiently light executive and model portraits, high and low key images, and more. Master traditional lighting styles and use creative modifications that will maximize your results. $29.95 list, 8½x11, 128p, 300 color photos, index, order no. 1778.

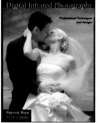

DIGITAL INFRARED
PHOTOGRAPHY

Patrick Rice

The dramatic look of infrared photography has long made it popular—but with digital it's actually *easy* too! Add digital IR to your repertoire with this comprehensive book. $29.95 list, 8½x11, 128p, 100 b&w and color photos, index, order no. 1792.

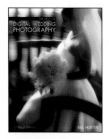

THE BEST OF DIGITAL
WEDDING PHOTOGRAPHY

Bill Hurter

Explore the groundbreaking images and techniques that are shaping the future of wedding photography. Includes dazzling photos from over 35 top photographers. $29.95 list, 8½x11, 128p, 175 color photos, index, order no. 1793.

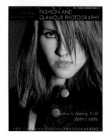

LIGHTING TECHNIQUES FOR
FASHION AND GLAMOUR
PHOTOGRAPHY

Stephen A. Dantzig, PsyD.

In fashion and glamour photography, light is the key to producing images with impact. With these techniques, you'll be primed for success! $29.95 list, 8½x11, 128p, over 200 color images, index, order no. 1795.

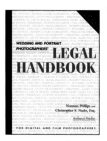

WEDDING AND PORTRAIT
PHOTOGRAPHERS'
LEGAL HANDBOOK

N. Phillips and C. Nudo, Esq.

Don't leave yourself exposed! Sample forms and practical discussions help you protect yourself and your business. $29.95 list, 8½x11, 128p, 25 sample forms, index, order no. 1796.

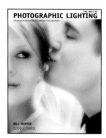

THE BEST OF
PHOTOGRAPHIC LIGHTING

Bill Hurter

Top professionals reveal the secrets behind their successful strategies for studio, location, and outdoor lighting. Packed with tips for portraits, still lifes, and more. $34.95 list, 8½x11, 128p, 150 color photos, index, order no. 1808.

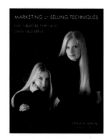

MARKETING &
SELLING TECHNIQUES

FOR DIGITAL PORTRAIT PHOTOGRAPHY

Kathleen Hawkins

Great portraits aren't enough to ensure the success of your business! Learn how to attract clients and boost your sales. $34.95 list, 8½x11, 128p, 150 color photos, index, order no. 1804.

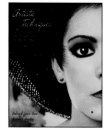

ARTISTIC TECHNIQUES WITH
ADOBE® PHOTOSHOP® AND
COREL® PAINTER®

Deborah Lynn Ferro

Flex your creative skills and learn how to transform photographs into fine-art masterpieces. Step-by-step techniques make it easy! $34.95 list, 8½x11, 128p, 200 color images, index, order no. 1806.

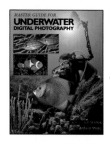

MASTER GUIDE FOR
UNDERWATER DIGITAL
PHOTOGRAPHY

Jack and Sue Drafahl

Make the most of digital! Jack and Sue Drafahl take you from equipment selection to underwater shooting techniques. $34.95 list, 8½x11, 128p, 250 color images, index, order no. 1807.

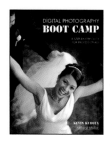

DIGITAL PHOTOGRAPHY
BOOT CAMP

Kevin Kubota

Kevin Kubota's popular workshop is now a book! A down-and-dirty, step-by-step course in building a professional photography workflow and creating digital images that sell! $34.95 list, 8½x11, 128p, 250 color images, index, order no. 1809.

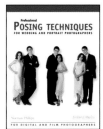

PROFESSIONAL POSING TECHNIQUES FOR WEDDING AND PORTRAIT PHOTOGRAPHERS

Norman Phillips

Master the techniques you need to pose subjects successfully—whether you are working with men, women, children, or groups. $34.95 list, 8½x11, 128p, 260 color photos, index, order no. 1810.

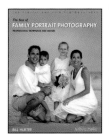

THE BEST OF FAMILY PORTRAIT PHOTOGRAPHY

Bill Hurter

Acclaimed photographers reveal the secrets behind their most successful family portraits. Packed with award-winning images and helpful techniques. $34.95 list, 8½x11, 128p, 150 color photos, index, order no. 1812.

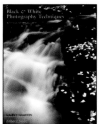

BLACK & WHITE PHOTOGRAPHY TECHNIQUES WITH ADOBE® PHOTOSHOP®

Maurice Hamilton

Become a master of the black & white digital darkroom! Covers all the skills required to perfect your black & white images and produce dazzling fine-art prints. $34.95 list, 8½x11, 128p, 150 color/b&w images, index, order no. 1813.

NIGHT AND LOW-LIGHT TECHNIQUES FOR DIGITAL PHOTOGRAPHY

Peter Cope

With even simple point-and-shoot digital cameras, you can create dazzling nighttime photos. Get started quickly with this step-by-step guide. $34.95 list, 8½x11, 128p, 100 color photos, index, order no. 1814.

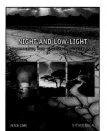

PROFESSIONAL MARKETING & SELLING TECHNIQUES FOR DIGITAL WEDDING PHOTOGRAPHERS, SECOND EDITION

Jeff Hawkins and Kathleen Hawkins

Taking great photos isn't enough to ensure success! Become a master marketer and salesperson with these easy techniques. $34.95 list, 8½x11, 128p, 150 color photos, index, order no. 1815.

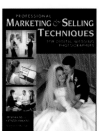

MASTER COMPOSITION GUIDE FOR DIGITAL PHOTOGRAPHERS

Ernst Wildi

Composition can truly make or break an image. Master photographer Ernst Wildi shows you how to analyze your scene or subject and produce the best-possible image. $34.95 list, 8½x11, 128p, 150 color photos, index, order no. 1817.

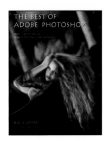

THE BEST OF ADOBE® PHOTOSHOP®

Bill Hurter

Rangefinder editor Bill Hurter calls on the industry's top photographers to share their strategies for using Photoshop to intensify and sculpt their images. No matter your specialty, you'll find inspiration here. $34.95 list, 8½x11, 128p, 170 color photos, 10 screen shots, index, order no. 1818.

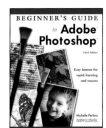

MASTER LIGHTING TECHNIQUES FOR OUTDOOR AND LOCATION DIGITAL PORTRAIT PHOTOGRAPHY

Stephen A. Dantzig

Use natural light alone or with flash fill, bare-bulb, and strobes to shoot perfect portraits all day long. $34.95 list, 8½x11, 128p, 175 color photos, diagrams, index, order no. 1821.

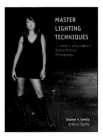

BEGINNER'S GUIDE TO ADOBE® PHOTOSHOP®, 3rd Ed.

Michelle Perkins

Enhance your photos, create original artwork, or add unique effects to any image. Topics are presented in easy-to-digest sections that will ensure outstanding images. $34.95 list, 8½x11, 128p, 80 color images, 120 screen shots, order no. 1823.

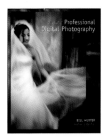

THE BEST OF PROFESSIONAL DIGITAL PHOTOGRAPHY

Bill Hurter

This book spotlights the methods that world-renowned photographers use to create their standout images. $34.95 list, 8½x11, 128p, 180 color photos, 20 screen shots, index, order no. 1824.

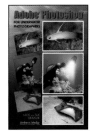

ADOBE® PHOTOSHOP® FOR UNDERWATER PHOTOGRAPHERS

Jack and Sue Drafahl

In this sequel to *Digital Imaging for the Underwater Photographer*, Jack and Sue Drafahl show you advanced techniques for solving a wide range of image problems that are unique to underwater photography. $39.95 list, 6x9, 224p, 100 color photos, 120 screen shots, index, order no. 1825.

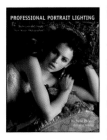

PROFESSIONAL PORTRAIT LIGHTING TECHNIQUES AND IMAGES FROM MASTER PHOTOGRAPHERS

Michelle Perkins

Get a behind-the-scenes look at the lighting techniques employed by the world's top portrait photographers. $34.95 list, 8½x11, 128p, 200 color photos, index, order no. 2000.

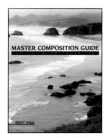

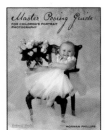

MASTER POSING GUIDE
FOR CHILDREN'S PORTRAIT PHOTOGRAPHY

Norman Phillips

Create perfect portraits of infants, tots, kids, and teens. Includes techniques for standing, sitting, and floor poses for boys and girls, individuals, and groups. $34.95 list, 8½x11, 128p, 305 color images, order no. 1826.

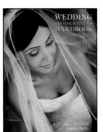

WEDDING PHOTOGRAPHER'S HANDBOOK

Bill Hurter

Learn to produce images with unprecedented technical proficiency and superb, unbridled artistry. Includes images and insights from top industry pros. $34.95 list, 8½x11, 128p, 180 color photos, 10 screen shots, index, order no. 1827.

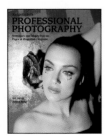

RANGEFINDER'S PROFESSIONAL PHOTOGRAPHY

edited by Bill Hurter

Editor Bill Hurter shares over one hundred "recipes" from *Rangefinder's* popular cookbook series, showing you how to shoot, pose, light, and edit fabulous images. $34.95 list, 8½x11, 128p, 150 color photos, index, order no. 1828.

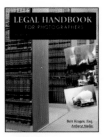

LEGAL HANDBOOK FOR PHOTOGRAPHERS, 2nd Ed.

Bert P. Krages, Esq.

Learn what you can and cannot photograph, how to handle conflicts should they arise, how to protect your rights to your images in the digital age, and more. $34.95 list, 8½x11, 128p, 80 b&w photos, index, order no. 1829.

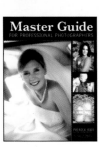

MASTER GUIDE
FOR PROFESSIONAL PHOTOGRAPHERS

Patrick Rice

Turn your hobby into a thriving profession. This book covers equipment essentials, capture strategies, lighting, posing, digital effects, and more, providing a solid footing for a successful career. $34.95 list, 8½x11, 128p, 200 color images, order no. 1830.

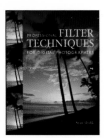

PROFESSIONAL FILTER TECHNIQUES
FOR DIGITAL PHOTOGRAPHERS

Stan Sholik

Select the best filter options for your photographic style and discover how their use will affect your images. $34.95 list, 8½x11, 128p, 150 color images, index, order no. 1831.

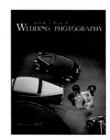

MASTER'S GUIDE TO WEDDING PHOTOGRAPHY
CAPTURING UNFORGETTABLE MOMENTS AND LASTING IMPRESSIONS

Marcus Bell

Learn to capture the unique energy and mood of each wedding and build a lifelong client relationship. $34.95 list, 8½x11, 128p, 200 color photos, index, order no. 1832.

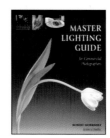

MASTER LIGHTING GUIDE
FOR COMMERCIAL PHOTOGRAPHERS

Robert Morrissey

Learn to use the tools and techniques the pros rely upon to land corporate clients. Includes diagrams, images, and techniques for a failsafe approach to creating shots that sell. $34.95 list, 8½x11, 128p, 110 color photos, 125 diagrams, index, order no. 1833.

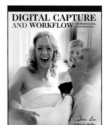

DIGITAL CAPTURE AND WORKFLOW
FOR PROFESSIONAL PHOTOGRAPHERS

Tom Lee

Cut your image-processing time by fine-tuning your workflow. Includes tips for working with Photoshop and Adobe Bridge, plus framing, matting, and more. $34.95 list, 8½x11, 128p, 150 color images, index, order no. 1835.